Marriage-Lite

Marriage-Lite
The Rise of Cohabitation and its Consequences

Patricia Morgan

Institute for the Study of Civil Society
London

First published August 2000

© The Institute for the Study of Civil Society 2000
email: books@civil-society.org.uk

ISBN 1-903 386-04-7

Typeset by the Institute for the Study of Civil Society
in New Century Schoolbook

Printed in Great Britain by
The Cromwell Press, Trowbridge, Wiltshire

Contents

The Author

Patricia Morgan, Senior Research Fellow at the Institute for the Study of Civil Society, is a sociologist specialising in criminology and family policy. Her books include *Delinquent Fantasies*, 1978; *Facing Up to Family Income,* 1989; *Families in Dreamland*, 1992; *Farewell to the Family?*, 1995; *Are Families Affordable?*, 1996; *Who Needs Parents?*, 1996; *Adoption And The Care of Children*, 1998; and *Adoption: The Continuing Debate*, 1999. She has contributed chapters to *Full Circle, Family Portraits, The Loss of Virtue, Tried But Untested, Liberating Women from Modern Feminism, Just a Piece of Paper?* and *The Fragmenting Family,* as well as articles for periodicals and national newspapers. Patricia Morgan is a frequent contributor to television and radio programmes and is presently writing a full-length work on the relationship between capitalism and the family.

Foreword

On 4 January 1994 the BBC launched the Year of the Family with a programme called *The Family Show*. In one section of it, the presenter Nick Ross asked childcare expert Penelope Leach for her views on the prospects for children born outside marriage, and her reply was illuminating:

> You said born outside marriage... What's that got to do with anything? There are no statistics whatsoever that suggest marriage—that piece of paper—makes any difference at all. What matters is relationships.

Penelope Leach was taking the line which still remains extremely popular amongst social policy intellectuals. Whilst it had become obvious that growing up with a lone parent put a child at a disadvantage, the alternative—according to the *bien-pensants*—was not to advocate marriage. Rather, it was seen as more 'inclusive' to say that, if a child has two parents, it matters little if they are married to each other, or even if both adults are the biological parents.

In 1994 Penelope Leach was right to say that there was very little, by way of statistical evidence, to prove anything about marriage *vis-a-vis* cohabitation, but we are now in a different situation. In 1999 Patricia Morgan returned to her 1995 classic, *Farewell to the Family?*, in order to prepare a second edition. She realised that, while there was a shortage of studies of cohabitation *per se*, it had become possible, in the years since the first edition of the book, to extract a good deal of information from other studies which cast light on the cohabiting lifestyle. This book is the result of collecting the evidence from this multiplicity of sources, and it has yielded some surprising results.

Far from being a mirror-image of marriage, cohabitation turns out to be something fundamentally different. Firstly, it is very fragile. Cohabiting relationships are always more likely to fracture than marriages entered into at the same time, regardless of age and income. It is no longer true that people cohabit until children come along and then tie the knot. Cohabitations with children are more likely to fragment than childless ones. Couples who have children and then marry are more likely to divorce than couples who have children within marriage, and couples who have children without getting married at all are highly unlikely to stay together while those children grow up.

Cohabitants behave more like single people than married people in a number of ways, notably in their attitudes towards fidelity to their partners. Cohabitation is sometimes presented as setting women free from the shackles of patriarchy. In fact the women and their children

are at greater risk of abuse than they would be in married relationships, and a number of the testimonies quoted in this books reveal
women to be very dissatisfied with their situations. The quality of
their relationships, to which Penelope Leach and others attach such
importance, is often very low indeed.

Radical critics of the family like to present the increase in cohabitation as a sign of rebellion against the restrictive old forms. As Patricia
Morgan shows, however, this conscious defiance of tradition is
characteristic of only a tiny number of cohabitants—the Bohemian
élite. For many people, cohabitation is not so much their ideal lifestyle
choice as the best arrangement they can make at the time. Opinion
polls consistently show marriage to be very popular. Increasing
numbers of divorces, single-parent families and people living alone do
not represent a triumph of the *avant-garde* so much as a failure by
individuals to achieve their goals in life. There is a gap between what
they want and what they get.

Patricia Morgan has outlined in other publications some possible
solutions to bridge this gap, but in this book she takes a very radical
stance indeed and speaks up for institutions:

> Institutions, whether marriage or private property, embody and sustain systems
> of meaning... and provide people with reference points outside their own
> consciousness that give coherence and continuity to their efforts. It is very
> difficult for people to cobble together their own lives, making up their own rules
> as they go along, and continually figuring out how everything is supposed to
> work (pp. 53-54).

Like private property and corporations, marriage depends on its legal
status to exist at all. In spite of this, we are witnessing increasingly
successful campaigns to transfer to cohabiting couples the legal rights
which used to belong to marriage, from travel passes for partners to
claims on property and the right to take decisions affecting children's
lives. There is an obvious contradiction here since, if people insist that
the state has no role to play in people's private lives, it is difficult to
understand why they should at the same time expect to be able to
invoke the law against their partners to establish their 'rights'.
Meanwhile, as the prerogatives of marriage drain away into the sump
of alternative lifestyles, so marriage itself becomes less attractive and
fewer people opt for it. The gap between what people want and what
they get widens, and we find more people living alone.

Groucho Marx once said that marriage is a great institution, but who
wants to live in an institution? The answer would seem to be that most
of us do, but many don't get the chance.

Perhaps the battle-cry of the new anti-establishment should be, let's
hear it for the institutions!

Robert Whelan

Introduction

The Received Wisdom

Cohabitation has shown a spectacular increase in a short period, occurring before marriage, after marriage, in between marriages and instead of marriage.

Cohabitation is an area where there is a need for more information, as—whether in policy making or in individual lives—decisions are being made on the basis of unexamined, and perhaps, erroneous assumptions. There is more knowledge now available, and it needs to be smuggled past the politically correct gatekeepers who dominate the organisations dealing with research and advice in the area of family affairs. With a little more light shed on this subject, then what people want and what they value may stand a better chance of being matched with what they get.

What 'Everyone Knows'

Presumptions abound about cohabitation, and there may be a very hit-and-miss relationship with reality. In a paper canvassing proposals to give unmarried fathers the same parental rights as married fathers, the Lord Chancellor's department states its belief that 'the growing acceptance of long-term cohabitation as a preliminary or alternative to marriage' means that: 'many such relationships must be at least as stable as marriage'.[1] Indeed, since large numbers of children are now born to unmarried parents, the guess is that 'many ...are likely to be in stable relationships'.[2] The Law Society believes, even more hopefully, that the simple increase in births outside marriage 'does suggest an increase in the number of stable unions outside marriage'.[3] In all cases, the axiomatic assumption is that the second follows from the first. There seems to be little or no inkling that evidence is relevant, let alone what the facts might be. The new Advisory Board on Family Law, appointed to respond to such government initiatives on family policy issues, followed suit. It did not consider that parental responsibility should be automatically conferred on all unmarried genitors, but only on those who sign the birth register along with the mother, as this already 'effectively constitutes a formal commitment to family life'.[4] If what sounds right has to be true, the same could be said about the Home Secretary Jack Straw's view that we 'shouldn't get in a paddy about the decline of formal marriage'. It seems that 'other kinds of families, including single-parent families, parents who live together without choosing to marry, and step-families, can do just as well for their children'—on the grounds that '...the most important thing is the quality of the relationship, not the institution in itself'.[5] The quality of the relationship may, indeed, be a 'most important thing' or proximate cause of how well parents do for their children (although it is not clear if what is meant is the parent/parent relationship or the parent/child relationship). However, it does not necessarily follow that the same 'quality of relationship' is equally distributed or present in all 'kinds of families'—and that, therefore, institutions themselves have no impact on relationship quality.

Politicians and government bodies are distilling the wisdom of academics and social commentators who have been prone to represent cohabitation as some folk or ethnic variant of marriage, minus the 'piece of paper', or 'one more modification in this range of living arrangements that are generically called marriage'.[6] These are apt to maintain that: 'there may be little to distinguish between the two types of union and there may be more variation within marriage and cohabiting unions than between them'. In turn, what differences there are 'are less to do with the private domain and more to do with their relationship to the institutional framework of society'[7]—something which favours cohabitation as the more progressive approach to intimate relationships. Cohabitation is even presented as marriage as we had it in the past. As such, it is 'a revival of... the private ordering of marriage, or social marriage' compared with 'enforced officially sanctioned ways of living'[8] which were imposed in a historically brief, recent and atypical period. This is located in Victorian times or, increasingly, the 1950s, to which the nuclear family, or two-parent family with formal marriage, is often consigned as some kind of aberrant or strange departure which foolish or nostalgic people mistake for the reality of family life before the 'changes' of recent decades. Thus:

> it is perhaps the 'rush to marry' which peaked in the 1950s that is unusual, rather than the growth in informal unions and the apparent loosening of the marriage tie that we are witnessing today.[9]

If the Home Secretary accepts that: 'In the last century... large numbers of people never went through formal ceremonies',[10] then he is drawing on claims that 'between the mid-eighteenth century and mid-nineteenth centuries as many as one-fifth of the population in England and Wales may have cohabited unlawfully for some period, either as a prelude to legal marriage or as a substitute for it' and even that from 'the 1750s onward rates of unmarried pregnancy and illegitimacy rose to levels unprecedented in recorded British history'.[11] Apparently, there was 'a veritable cornucopia of informal marriage practices' before the unfortunate interregnum of the 1950s. This involved couples jumping over broomsticks ('besom weddings') or entering into 'living tally' to 'create lives that made sense, that suit their own preferences and circumstances, rather than those of church and state'.

The attack on the family has been the most obvious, enduring and successful expression of the counter-cultural revolution. As the hated 'patriarchy' is defined as the 'manifestation and institutionalisation of male dominance over women and children in the family and the extension of male dominance over women in society in general',[12] so the 'significant family tie is the sexual affiliation that, when legally sanctioned, creates marriage'.[13] With marriage seen as restrictive and confining, destroying independence and autonomy, it easily appears that the unencumbered life is the one without binding commitments. Thus, it is cohabitation which affords people choice to determine their own conditions for the establishment and dissolution of relationships. Marriage, as such, particularly limits the self-development and determination of women. And, while marriage dictates feelings, emotions and behaviour, cohabitation is a form of liberation from traditional values and oppressive structures. Marriage requires respect and obedience to an institution, or the structure of the relationship, and seems to give the state and the church the right to interfere in personal life, militating against the development of the partners' mutual understanding and love, and undermining their emotional bonds and personal growth.

According to Anthony Giddens, progressive guru of the 'third way', the increasing separation of sexuality from the realities of reproduction (and reproduction from sexuality by technological developments) has separated it from all institutional and normative control and made it simply a vehicle for self-expression and self-actualisation.[14] Such 'plastic' (sic) sexuality as part of the 'project of self' is realised in 'pure relationships' which are organised and sustained primarily from within themselves, being unsupported, unregulated and unconstrained by any external social standards, laws, conventions or rules. Entered into for their own sake, they are continued only in so far as the relationship is thought by each individual to deliver enough satisfactions. What '...holds the pure relationship together is the acceptance on the part of each partner, "until further notice", that each gains sufficient benefit from the relationship to make its continuance worthwhile'.[15] Such a 'transformation of intimacy' as Giddens sees happening is a fulfilment of the dreams of Herbert Marcuse and Wilhelm Reich for complete sexual emancipation. The difference is that, while these sexual radicals who inspired the 1960s counter-culture saw a version of the Marxist revolution, or overthrow of capitalism by socialism, as the essential prerequisite, Giddens sees the 'advancement of self-autonomy in the context of pure relationships' or 'the democratisation of personal life' going hand in hand with the development of democracy in the wider community and even 'in the global political order at the most extensive level'.[16] Complete autonomy is essential to democracy, which means the 'capacity of individuals to be self-reflective and self-determining: to deliberate, judge, choose and act upon different possible courses of action'. Each person must freely and equally determine and regulate the conditions of their association and own lives, in order to provide for the elaboration of individuality. This 'reflexive project of self' must be developed in such a fashion as permits autonomy in relation to the past, whence people might 'colonise' or construct the future entirely in their own fashion. Moreover, the process is already underway 'from the bottom up', involving a wide-ranging emotional reorganisation of social life, and a radical democratisation of the personal.

Marriage is seen to be veering increasingly towards the form of a pure relationship.[17] However, while Giddens finds that:

> ...marriage 'in the traditional sense' is disappearing, it is the gays who are the pioneers in this respect—the prime everyday experimenters.[18]

And, while marriages are still more difficult to dissolve than gay relationships, cohabitation among heterosexuals better approximates to the 'pure relationship' which is in line with modernity. However, unlike other official or academic sources, Giddens does not pretend that this is both more free or informal than marriage, yet somehow 'indistinguishable' or 'just as stable'. Instead, the lack of external constraints, anchorage or guidelines makes cohabitation inherently unstable and more apt to disintegrate.

Without marriage to create obligations between the adult parties, their kin, and the couple and their children, there is the prospect of a one-generational society. Cohabitation is at odds with reproduction or childrearing, for, unless children are going to contribute to the self-actualisation of the adults involved, they are a potential threat to the 'pure relationship'. Hence, freedom involves ridding ourselves of the claims of childhood as the *sine qua non* for the family. While Giddens 'democratisation of personal life, as a potential, extends in a funda-mental way to... the relations of parents, children and other kin', how are children meant to survive and thrive as '[i]ndividuals involved in determining the conditions of their association', exploiting 'the democratising possibilities of the transformation of intimacy'?[19] In contrast, marriage is an institution with a public dimension, which brings what are initially non-kin relations—but ones vital to the creation and maintenance of further kin relationships—into their moral ambit. Moreover, the particular patterns of sentiments, values and action that are generated in family and kinship relations and are distinctive of this domain, also work to maintain the trust and solidarity underlying all social relationships. In this respect marriage is not only pivotal in producing ties of kinship which are necessary for social bonds, but is also the crucible of the social values we all rely on: loyalty, commitment, truthfulness, promise-keeping, self-discipline and service.[20]

However, whether cohabitation is seen as marriage under another name or not, the policy implications are the same. The dominant idea is that:

> Contractual commitment to a child [is]... separated from marriage, and made by each parent as a binding matter of law, with unmarried and married fathers having the same rights and the same obligations. ...such a restructuring of parenthood would undermine the very idea of the 'single parent'.[21]

People would move in and out of sexual relationships, but somehow continue to 'parent' children in the same or different households. Indeed, it is possible that we are already at this point, where:

> ...having a child is an altogether different decision from in the past... The proportion of children born outside marriage probably won't decline, and lifelong sexual partnerships will almost certainly become increasingly uncommon.[22]

This puts cohabitants in the lead, as the expression of 'the new model' and 'alternative ground' on which to base family relationships. Cohabitation is 'outgrowing marriage in importance'.[23]

Chapter 1

Who Wants To Be A Cohabitee?

Who Wants To Cohabit?

Cohabitation seems a good way to have some of the benefits of marriage while preparing for marriage or, at least, an opportunity for those who do not feel ready for the demands of marriage to enjoy the advantages of sexual co-residence. Couples can learn about each other as they share expenses, and see if the partner makes an acceptable mate.[1] If they prove incompatible, then breaking up seems easy to do, without legal formalities and personal loss. It is generally assumed that, as 'cohabitation weeds out unsuitable partners through a process of natural de-selection... perhaps after several living-together relationships, a person will eventually find a marriageable mate'.[2] It is also widely believed that:

> cohabitants benefit from living together unmarried in personal and in social terms... especially in terms of the quality of a subsequent marriage: trial cohabitation is believed to provide ideal conditions for establishing a successful relationship, and a 'better' marriage.[3]

In other words, it is an 'enriched courtship'. In contrast, 'traditional courtship as a way of finding out about a person's character' is reflected 'as a "game", full of artifice and role-playing, while living together is more natural, honest and revealing'.[4]

Some parting of the ways is evident between the public on one side and officials, politicians and academics on the other, when it comes to equating cohabitation with marriage in status, or in preferring this to marriage. As cohabitation, particularly preceding marriage, has leapt upward, making it possible to ask how it has happened 'that what was morally reprehensible has become the majority experience in just two decades',[5] marriage itself has persistently enjoyed overwhelming public support. Such is public conservatism in belief and practice that Anthony Giddens, in the 1999 Reith lectures, complained that he finds 'the persistence of the traditional family... more worrying than its decline'.

The consistent return from opinion samples shows that around 90 per cent of young people want to marry and most want children. Indeed, there are indications on both sides of the Atlantic that having a good marriage as a life goal has, if anything, increased in importance, and for the young.[6] While 43 per cent of British respondents to international surveys in the late 1980s would advise a young woman to live with a partner and then marry (compared to 26 per cent in the US), only four per cent would advise living with a steady partner without marrying (three per cent in the US).[7] Moreover, while two out of three people under 45 advised young people to cohabit before marriage, the great majority still recommended that the cohabiting union be converted to marriage (only five per cent approved cohabiting only). A Mori poll, ten years later, gave the preferred lifestyle of 65 per cent of men and 71 per cent of women as 'being married with children'. Only four per cent of men and three per cent of women nominated 'being unmarried with a partner and children', and living by oneself with children was favoured by one per cent of men and four per cent of women—although 75 per cent of people disagreed that a single, pregnant woman *should* marry the father. Men were more likely than women to want to be childless and 'partnered' rather than married—a point to which I shall return. (Being unmarried with a partner and no children was preferred by nine per cent of men and four per cent of women, and being married with no children by ten per cent of men and seven per cent of women.) Moreover, the proportion believing that marriage should be permanent has increased over the 1990s.[8] A study of cohabitation breakdown by Carol Smart and Pippa Stevens showed men more inclined to be opposed to marriage than women, but emphasise that this was more because men saw it as an irrelevance than because they held strong ideological positions 'as part of some kind of grassroots social movement wishing to challenge the institution for political or ideological reasons'. Indeed, good tax or social security reasons would sway them in the opposite direction. Any expressed ideological opposition, from men or women, was hopelessly confused, and to do with, for example, 'being somewhat of a hippie'; 'it [marriage] was about Christianity and things like that'; or 'she was living in this housing co-op, which sort of, [sic] green housing co-op with social change ideals'.[9]

Unsurprisingly, public attitudes are contradictory, and it is difficult to distinguish the need to appear tolerant and unbiased from beliefs about similarities (or differences) in relationships. The new National Family and Parenting Institute proudly launched itself with the findings of a Mori poll which showed that only one in five parents felt that being married was very important to children's happiness (and only one in ten in the 25-44 age group: 'suggesting that persuading people that marriage is central is preaching to the unconverted').[10] With marriage not thought 'crucial to "good" childrearing', the Institute is cheered by the way in which young 'parents placed more emphasis on children feeling loved and cared for... They were also more interested in parents getting on well together'. However, preaching to the unconverted has to be distinguished from informing the ignorant. Beliefs about the irrelevance of marriage to good childrearing, or to parents getting on well together and children being loved and cared for, like those about the efficacy of cohabitation to create good long-term relationships, are empirical matters whose veracity depends upon evidence. Public support or approval for cohabitation rest largely upon assumptions about utility that are open to confirmation or refutation on the basis of available data. The National Family and Parenting Institute purports to be an educational body, founded by the government to 'enhance the value and quality of family life, to make sure than parents are supported in bringing up their children and in finding the help and information they need'. This role seems to have been speedily identified in terms of the endorsement and furtherance of beliefs on the basis of their political correctness, rather than factual foundation.

From Bohemia To The Mainstream

The modern advance of cohabitation is often described as one where, in the first stage of social transition, this is an *avant garde* phenomenon practised by a small bohemian élite: most people marry directly. In the second stage cohabitation becomes a widely accepted and practised prelude to marriage and is predominantly a childless phase, so that what 'started as a protest against bourgeois marriage ... changed into a means of gradual movement into a union, whereas direct marriage changed from being normal to being deviant'.[11] In the third stage cohabitation becomes an acceptable alternative to marriage and parenthood is no longer restricted to marriage.

In a *hypothesised* fourth stage, supposedly reached in Scandinavia, 'cohabitation and marriage become indistinguishable with children being born and reared within both, and the partnership transition could be said to be complete'.[12] In 1996, according to the Eurobarometer data, 45 per cent of Danish women, and 39 per cent of Swedish women aged 20-24, cohabited (compared to 13 per cent in Britain), and 35 per cent and 33 per cent respectively of 25-29-year-olds (compared with 12 per cent in Britain).[13] This fourth stage is highly contentious, even if this often seems to have assumed the status of a guiding reality, or basis for action. Moreover, some injustice may be done to the complexities and possibilities of cohabitation if this is seen simply as a precursor or substitute for marriage. It may develop in other directions and, for example, encroach backwards into courtship and dating.[14]

The first stage, while seemingly unproblematic, may also be disputed. While cohabitation among the Bohemian intelligentsia may have been an ostentatious political statement, it was probably as or more common among less educated groups up into the 1950s, while still affecting only a small minority. From then, it increased among all groups even if, again, it was more obvious among the college or university educated.[15] Since cohabitants are more likely than married couples both to be both working or both unemployed, this can be used to illustrate how cohabitation has developed from two socially opposite origins, the educated élite and the lower class.[16] For Australia, Sotirios Sarantakos speaks of trial, liberal and *de facto* cohabitation (where marriage is avoided more for practical and economic reasons than because the participants are against marriage on principle, or trying out the relationship). The latter is found more among those of poor educational level, while participants in trial or liberal cohabitation are skewed towards the higher educational strata.[17]

Cohabitation now typically initiates a first union for men and women in the Western European and Nordic countries. In the mid-1960s, five per cent of never-married women cohabited before marriage in Great Britain. By the 1990s, around 70 per cent in their first marriages had cohabited with their future spouse.[18] The suggestion is that, when it comes to people under 35 now entering first partnerships, 79 per cent of men and 71 per cent of women cohabit.[19] Pre-marital cohabitation is particularly common before second or subsequent marriages: among remarrying women it is around 90 per cent. By 1998, 12 per cent of men and 11 per cent of women under 60 in Great Britain were cohabiting.[20] In younger age groups, more women in 'live-in partnerships' are cohabiting than are married, or 55 per cent of those aged 20-24 in 1995 (compared with 11 per cent in 1980).[21] Unmarried men and women (single and divorced) aged 25-34 have the highest rates of cohabitation, of 40 and 34 per cent respectively.[22]

In the 1990s the largest increases have been occurring among those over 30, particularly those aged 35-40. While the numbers are expected to rise for all ages, predictions are that this will continue to be much greater among the over-35s.[23]

Never-married cohabitants with children represent about one in four of all never-married cohabiting couples.[24] About a half of post-marital cohabitants will be in 'step-families', with children from one or more previous marriages, and sometimes additional children of the couple. The proportion of families with dependent children headed by an unmarried couple increased from five to 11 per cent between 1986 and 1994.[25] (However, it must be remembered that, in 1994, married-couple families still accounted for 71 per cent of those with dependent children.) Around a half of first births outside marriage in England and Wales are probably born into cohabitational unions (or 58 per cent of these in 1996), being jointly registered and giving the same address.

In turn, around three in ten of never-married mothers may be cohabiting at any one time, which might or might not be in the relationship that originally produced the child(ren).[26] In the US, around a third of the unmarried births to non-Hispanic whites are to cohabiting couples; the rate being far lower for black women (who are more likely to be living alone) and higher for Mexican Americans.

As the increase in cohabitation has been accompanied by a decline in marriage, in terms of both marriages postponed and marriages foregone, this raises questions of how much one is replacing the other to any degree, and whether or not it connotes rejection of marriage *per se*. As it is, marriage rates have fallen considerably at younger ages, without any sign of compensating increases in the older age groups. In 1971, 80 per cent of women were married by the age of 25, but in 1990 half were single, with the average age in Britain at first marriage rising from 23 to 27 years for women and from 25 to 29 years for men by 1996. Over the last two decades the number of males who had never been married by the age of 29 has grown from 26 per cent to a half. In 1960, for every thousand single men over 16, 77 got married for the first time. In 1970 it was 86. In 1991 it was 37 and in 1996, 29.8. Projections are that the proportion of adults who have never married will rise from 32 per cent in 1996 to 41 per cent in 2021 for males, and from 24 per cent to 33 per cent for females. When the effects of divorce are added, the proportion of the population that is married may fall to around 45 per cent by 2021.[27]

Declining rates of remarriage following divorce and lengthening intervals between divorce and remarriage are widely attributable to increased cohabitation. However, it cannot be assumed that the overall decline in marriage is just to do with its *replacement* by cohabitation, as there has been a decline in the proportions of people both forming partnerships or living in one at any particular point in time. The contraction of the conjugal family is faster than the advance of any 'alternatives'. Cohabiting couples with children may have grown by six per cent between 1986 and 1994, but married-couple families fell 12 per cent. A result was that one in ten men aged 25 to 44 was living alone in 1994, three times the proportion of 1973. Moreover, just as the substitution of cohabitation is hardly the only factor behind the fall in marriage, so cohabitation may be an important engine behind marital decline for reasons other than that it simply replaces marriage.

The rise of cohabitation has been placed in the context of the 'second demographic transition' where, as a flexible or temporary alternative to marriage, it has been made possible by such factors as highly efficient contraception and acceptance of recreational sex. Cohabitation has also been related to a general confrontation or challenge to all forms of institutional authority or external morality[28] which welled up in the mid-1960s, which 'has had "freedom of choice" as its theme and the acceptance of "alternative lifestyles" as its message'.[29] If this means that cohabitation has been part of some kind of radical protest against marriage, or principled rejection of the nuclear family, then this applies to no more than a small élite. As Sarantakos observed of his Australian sample of cohabitants, gathered in the later 1970s and early 1980s, the majority of respondents (or 82 per cent) saw cohabitation as a way of achieving companionship and convenience, be it social, economic, or personal, while few (13 per cent) were convinced that it was a form of liberation from traditional ways of life, or revolt against the established institutions, of which marriage was a part.[30]

This is not to deny that there may be an increasingly '...individualistic ethic [which] encourages us to think egocentrically about relationships ("what seems good for me")...' As people ask: 'Will I find full satisfaction in this relationship? If you can't give me what I want then I'll have to look elsewhere', so cohabitation seems to offer greater independence and economic control, combined with the ease of separating if the partner does not fulfil one's needs.[31]

As the sexual revolution, facilitated by innovations in contraceptive technology, made informal or consensual partnering viable, so 'acquiring education, establishing careers, indulging consumption tastes and pursuing leisure interests and travel aspirations'[32] could be combined with 'live-in', as much as other, sexual relationships. At the same time, the opportunity costs of remaining unmarried have been much reduced as sexual companionship has become routinely available to the single. Increasing economic uncertainty among the young, with deteriorating prospects for many young males, where the passage into adulthood has generally become more complex, unpredictable and attenuated, has discouraged early marriage. In a more complicated transition to adulthood, young people now spend substantial time living away from their families before marriage. With divorce on demand, illegitimate children equal with legitimate children, and unmarried mothers equated with married mothers,

> the growth of cohabitation and similar lifestyles is inevitable and indisputable. Why marry if companionship and children can be found outside this highly demanding and 'restrictive' institution? [of marriage] Or, as one respondent put it, why buy a cow if you can get the milk for nothing?[33]

The persistence of a strong popular desire for lifelong, loving marriage has been accompanied by mounting pessimism about the chances of attaining this. This erosion of confidence in lasting marriage has served to underline the popularly accepted rationale for cohabitation—that it is a way to test out compatibility and, upon break-up, a means to pre-empt the trauma of divorce, and separate without complications. In particular, first-hand experience—through divorce—of the fragility of contemporary marriage, with the:

> consequent wariness of precipitating marriage, and growing community tolerance of cohabitation, largely explain the expanded role of informal repartnering among the divorced and separated.[34]

In both cases, fear is engendered by 'no-fault' grounds that make divorce so easy, and the accompanying property settlements which enable the abusive, deserting or adulterous partner to walk away with half or more of the assets. As these will also be independent of who contributed what in the first place, the prospect of loss will figure increasingly strongly as young adults face marriage later, with more individual assets.[35] Girls who have been exposed to domestic violence in the parental generation generally wish not to get married and, should they make any relationships, these would preferably be without legal ties, which they assume will be easier to escape.[36]

Chapter 2

A Fragile And Transitory State

A Stable Relationship?

The most striking—and most often unappreciated—fact about cohabitation (apart from its growth) is that it tends to be short-lived. From the British Household Panel Study, it seems that just over a half of cohabitations of 3,273 women born since 1930 (who reported having at least one partnership), turned into marriage, while nearly 30 per cent dissolved.[1] This is in tune with the experience of the 1958 British birth cohort (in the National Child Development Study) where, by age 33, almost two-thirds of those whose first sexual, live-in relationship was a cohabitation had married their partner, 28 per cent had broken down and just eight per cent were still intact.[2]

Overall, the median duration of a childless cohabitation is 19 months, before it leads to a birth, a marriage or terminates.[3] By three years, three-quarters of women in the British Household Panel Study either had a birth, got married or dissolved the union. The median duration of all cohabitations involving never-married women is just under two years, and less than four per cent of cohabiting unions last ten years or more.[4] This matches cross-sectional data from the General House-hold Survey, which showed that, by the time they were interviewed, over a half of female cohabitants under 60 had lived with their partner for less than two years, and only 16 per cent for more than five years.[5] (Cross-sectional, rather than longitudinal, studies can give the impression that cohabitations last longer than is actually the case, since these pick up more 'survivors' by dipping into the population at one particular time, rather than following a sample over a period.)

Although a greater proportion of US cohabitations end in marriage, a similar picture pertains for America.[6] At prime ages of union-formation—from age 25 to 34—between 20 and 24 per cent of unmarried adults are cohabiting. About 45 per cent of the cohabitations of those in the US National Longitudinal Survey of Youth ended either in marriage or dissolution by the first year, 70 per cent by the second year and 90 per cent by five years. The median duration is about 15 months, with two-thirds of those in first cohabitations subsequently marrying their partner by four years.[7] Again, as longer cohabitations tend to 'accumulate' in the population, 20 per cent of cohabiting couples have lived together for five years or more.[8] The Australian Family Formation Project also found that a quarter of cohabitations lasted only 12 months, around a half of cohabitations have ended after two years in either dissolution or marriage, and three-quarters by four years.[9]

If we look only at cohabitations that do not convert to marriage, it seems that they are about four times more likely to break down than marriages. In the European Family and Fertility Surveys the survival of such cohabitations for women aged 20-39 years is that 18 per cent endure for ten years in Britain, compared to Switzerland at 25 per cent, with Norway, Spain, and Sweden in the 30 to 40 per cent range. Austria, France, Finland and West Germany lie between 40 to 50 per cent.[10] In Sarantakos' Australian sample, 8.7 per cent of the cohabitants still lived in their original cohabitation unit ten years later, while the proportion of their married counterparts was 71 per cent.[11]

We know that the younger the partners are at marriage, the higher the chances of breakdown but, interestingly, this does not explain the higher rate of dissolution for cohabitation compared to marriage. Over Europe,[12] the age at first partnership does not make much difference to the propensity of cohabitations that do not convert to marriage to be the most unstable of partnerships. In the British Household Panel Study, it seems that three per cent of couples in their first marriage experienced a separation over a three year period, compared to 20 per cent of cohabiting couples. Again, the stability of cohabiting unions did not seem to be related to the age at which they were formed, suggesting that these are 'intrinsically more fragile than marriage regardless of age at start of the partnership'.[13]

Over time, cohabitations have become less likely to lead to marriage —and thus more likely to be a prelude to separation. While twice as many relationships used to end in marriage rather than separation, now this is being reversed, as under a half of British women born after 1962 converted their union into marriage before having children, compared with three-fifths of those born earlier. Having a child has now become far more common for younger groups: 18 per cent of cohabiting women born after 1962 had unwed births compared to nine per cent of the previous 1950-62 cohort.[14] Similar trends are recorded for Canada, the United States and Australia.[15] In 1997, 36 per cent of all American unmarried households included a child under 18, up from 21 per cent in 1987. For the 25-34 age group the proportion approaches a half.[16] Moreover, the proportion of British women who legalise their union after having a child within a cohabiting union is low compared to other nationalities. In the European Family and Fertility Surveys it was around one-third by five years after the birth (while, in Switzerland, Austria, Italy and Sweden it was around 70 per cent).[17]

A Commitment To Family Life?

When we hear of cohabitations being 'stable unions', this usually refers to ones producing children, and this is assumed to be evidenced by couples registering the birth from the same address. However, less than one in ten British women having their first child in cohabitation are still cohabiting ten years on, or only 8.7 per cent. Just over a third would have married by five years and two-fifths by ten years,[18] but a half will be lone unmarried mothers because their relationships have dissolved. The low overall proportion of mothers who are cohabiting at any one time, compared with the large numbers of women who enter such relationships, is the result of the short duration of cohabitations— even given that longer cohabitations accumulate in the population.

It seems that only three in ten mothers who jointly registered the birth with the father from the same address in 1988 went on to marry in the subsequent eight years, a figure not very different from the one in four who registered the birth from different addresses.[19] Overall, one in four women who had an unwed birth married, and around three-quarters of these appeared to have married the father. These findings suggest that having different or the same addresses may be as indicative of the age of the mother as much or more than of the nature of her relationship with the father, 'committed', 'stable', or otherwise. Younger women were most likely to marry the father, whether they lived with him or not, and many did not live with him because they were presumably still at the parental home. In one small-scale study of cohabitation breakdown, a third of fathers had partners who experienced an unplanned pregnancy prior to cohabitation. This was what pushed them into the cohabitation, even though some may have hardly known their partners, who often resented the pregnancy as a trap.[20]

> It was her who fell pregnant without saying—especially, I think—loads of times, I thought she'd caught me, you know what I mean, so I was just against her having any more—just add more onto me. [The second child] wasn't agreed neither. She fell pregnant and she was born.

> ...he was quite reluctant, he did not want children, he was very clear about that, he did'nt want any children. So we both sort of really tried in a very difficult situation, but it wasn't going to work. It was never going to work.[21]

For over half of the women, it was unlikely that the cohabitation would have started if they had not become pregnant and few wanted to risk marrying their partner, because he was so obviously lacking as husband material. They gave up on the idea of eventual marriage when they realised that the man was unlikely ever to become more marriage-worthy, and that they were better off with someone else or on their own. Such mothers were initially keen on joint registration because they hoped it would bind the men to their children. 'Shotgun' weddings seem to have been replaced by 'shotgun' cohabitations, which have shorter life-spans.

Cohabitations which produce children are unions which are more likely to dissolve eventually, compared to childless cohabitations, because when a woman becomes a mother, this actually reduces the chances of her marrying the father.[22] The odds of marriage (relative to not marrying) for women who had their youngest child within cohabitation are 67 per cent lower than for childless women in the British Household Panel Study. While cohabitations with children have a slightly lower dissolution rate than those of childless women, ultimately more of these unions dissolve compared to those of childless women, simply because less are converted into marriage. Marriage rates for cohabiting couples have also been falling in the US, where the proportion of cohabiting mothers who eventually marry the child's father declined from 57 per cent to 44 per cent over the decade from 1987 to 1997. Thus: 'childbearing within cohabiting unions does not signal longer-term commitments' even if it does 'signal longer cohabitations'.[23]

It is couples in poorer financial circumstances who are not only less likely to marry, but more likely to have a baby, and the same applies to less educated women.[24] Better educated women are less likely to have a birth in a union before marriage. The incidence of single parenthood among never-married, childless women entering their first cohabitation is about halved amongst those who have achieved qualifications at A-level or above, relative to those with no qualifications. However, if they do have a birth in a cohabitation, the union is more likely to dissolve.

If anything, women from more affluent backgrounds are more likely to cohabit, but less likely to have a child in cohabitation, with middle-class women remaining single longer. A first birth within a cohabiting union in Britain is more likely when the man does not have a job, just as women whose fathers were in unskilled or semi-skilled manual jobs are much more likely to become mothers in cohabiting unions.[25]

Cohabiting couples with children are generally more likely to be of low socio-economic status compared to childless cohabitants, as well as married couples with children, when cross-sectional data is considered. (Remember that this picks up 'survivors' or more 'long-termers' compared to longitudinal studies, involving cohabitations that have persisted as such, rather than dissolved or converted to marriages.) An exception is Ros Pickford's very recent comparison of married and cohabiting fathers, where there were hardly any differences in this small sample, apart from the fact that cohabiting fathers were not so likely to have been educated beyond age 16.[26] In the British Family Resources Survey, 32 per cent of the younger male cohabitants with children received the basic benefit compared with 13 per cent of married fathers, and in the older group it was 22 compared with eight per cent. Average weekly income for younger cohabiting men under 39 with children was almost a third lower than for married fathers, who also had significantly higher hourly wage rates.[27] Over a half of cohabiting mothers in one study of 1992 had household incomes in the lowest ranges (18 per cent of cohabiting couples with children had net incomes of less than £6,000, compared with six per cent of women who married before having children). A quarter of these longer-term cohabitants lived in households where nobody was employed and one-fifth had a partner who had been unemployed for over two years.[28] Similar results were obtained from General Household Survey data of 1989, where 23 per cent of cohabiting couples with children had gross weekly incomes of less than £100 compared to six per cent of married parents. While 93 per cent of men in married-couple families were working, this applied to only 77 per cent of male cohabitants with children. In Mavis Maclean's and John Eekelaar's study,[29] many more of the formerly married fathers were employed before separation than the former cohabitants (or 77 per cent in full-time work as against only 55 per cent of the former cohabitants). This is lower than the 93 per cent for all married fathers with dependent children given for 1989, and is consistent with the evidence that marital breakdown rises as men's employment falls.[30]

The picture is similar in other English-speaking countries. In Australian data, 20 per cent of cohabiting couples with children received unemployment benefits in the year preceding the study compared to three per cent of married couples with children.[31] In New Zealand, cohabiting parents are less likely to be working, or 13 per cent of fathers and 46 per cent of mothers in 1991 compared to seven and 36 per cent of married fathers and mothers. Neither was working in 9.4 of cases, compared to 4.5 per cent for married couples. Twenty-seven per cent of fathers in cohabiting relationships and 18 per cent of mothers received the unemployment benefit at some time in the year prior to the 1991 census, compared with ten per cent of married fathers and seven per cent of married mothers. Family support—a means-tested benefit for low-income families—was paid to over a third or 34 per cent of cohabiting mothers, compared with 18 per cent of married mothers. Unsurprisingly, over a third (35 per cent), of cohabitants fell into the lowest income quintile, almost twice as many as the proportion of families where the parents were married (18 per cent). The representation of cohabitants declines progressively through the higher quintiles, with just 11 per cent in the top quintile, compared to 21 per cent of married-couple families (this is without equivalisation of incomes, or allowance for numbers, where cohabitants tend to have fewer children than married couples).

While, in the US, the 1996 poverty rate for children living in married-couple households was six per cent, it was 31 per cent for children living in cohabiting households, much closer to the rate of 45 per cent for children living with lone mothers.[32] Around a quarter of children in cohabiting families, like 30 per cent of those with single mothers, had mothers who received public assistance. One quarter of children in white, cohabiting-couple families live in poverty—four times greater than white children in married-couple families. On average, cohabiting couples with children have only about two-thirds of the income of married couples with children, mainly due to the fact that the average income of male cohabiting partners was only about a half of that of married male partners.

A selection effect is probably present, as the less well-off cohabit rather than marry. Marriage rates among men appear to be strongly influenced by wage rates, and the economic correlates of cohabitation and marriage relate almost exclusively to the position of the male partner. For the US, men's earnings fell by 20 per cent between 1972 and 1989, and marriage rates followed a roughly parallel course.[33] It has been estimated that a $100 increase in the weekly earnings of black men raised the odds of marriage by about 30 per cent for those aged 20-24 and by about 20 per cent for bachelors aged between 30-39. The employment and earnings effects for white men were remarkably similar in every age group.[34] However, economic differences between married and cohabiting parents persist for the US even when factors like parental education, race, parental age and age of children are considered. As we shall see, when men marry, especially when they have children, they tend to become more productive and responsible; working and earning more than their unmarried counterparts.[35] Another factor is the private transfer of wealth, particularly from older in-laws, which is considerably lower for cohabiting, compared to married, couples.[36] Family members are clearly less willing to transfer wealth to 'boyfriends', than to 'in-laws'. Paul R. Amato and Alan Booth also suggest that part of the reason for the inverse relationship between social class and cohabitation is that high-status and high-resource parents, concerned perhaps at the possible loss or 'leakage of wealth', discourage their children from cohabiting and put pressure upon cohabiting offspring either to marry or break up.[37]

The passage into marriage from cohabitation is associated with financial resources or labour market advantage, and as people acquire assets which they can bequeath, or something to transact, such as houses, savings and pensions. In their sample of 694 'women-year' observations, John Ermisch and Marco Francesconi,[38] observed how women in employment, like those with a partner in a job, were not only less likely to dissolve their union, but more likely to marry than those not in a job, or with an unemployed partner. Unexpected improvements in finances generally precipitated marriage. On average, the earnings of women (and the earnings of their partners) were lowest for women who dissolved their union, and highest for those who married. The differences were not great, except in the case of the male partner's earnings, where those with higher earnings significantly increased the chances of the union being converted to marriage and reduced the chances of dissolution. Along similar lines, Australian research showed how being employed reduced the risk of first cohabitation for women, while increasing the chances of first marriage.[39]

If a couple receive income support, the main means-tested benefit, they not only have a higher rate of dissolution, but a lower marriage rate. Means-tested benefits may discourage marriage, and encourage more low-income people to keep unions 'off the books', as these discriminate against officially or publicly recognised couples and make it financially worthwhile for people to operate as two singles, one with children. Family credit, and now working families tax credit, for the working poor, pays as much to a lone parent as to a couple on the same original wage, thus giving the couple a lower *per capita* income. If the mother operates as a lone parent, the father's wage or benefit is additional, and not counted against her entitlements. Many women in Carol Smart's and Pippa Stevens' study had kept their council tenancies in their own names, not only to preserve their housing security in the eventuality of a break-up, but because they did not wish it to appear to Social Security that they were cohabiting. They ensured that the male 'partner' had a different address.[40]

Cohabiting relationships tend to dissolve where they do not succumb to the incentives and intentions to form long-term unions. One or both may be missing, in a relationship where the connection between marriage and resources works both ways. While cohabiting men may tend to have poorer or more uncertain economic circumstances or prospects than married men, and while marriage also motivates men and makes them more productive, men have got to be willing, as much as able, to meet the demands of marriage. In Ros Pickford's sample, marriage to the child's mother was not considered by 44 per cent of the unmarried fathers because they thought marriage irrelevant or were apathetic, and by another 41 per cent because their relationship was unsatisfactory (the rest had had bad experiences with a previous or a parental marriage).[41] Those more favourably inclined towards marriage may well have done this before the child arrived. Many cohabiting men may be:

> only agreeing to 'share' family work with their partners so long as there were no children. They were neither keen to have them nor relished the additional ties and responsibilities.[42]

In Australian comparisons of 18-34-year-old married and cohabiting persons, never-married men (and previously-married women) were prominent among those both most likely to resist the formalisation of consensual unions and to report pressure from their partner to have children.[43]

Parental relationships in cohabiting groups seem to be significantly less established before the conception of a child than in married groups. The average length of a couple's relationship before the birth of their first child in Ros Pickford's sample was 30 per cent longer among the married, compared to the cohabiting, group of parents. Moreover, three-quarters of the cohabiting fathers, compared to under a half of the married fathers, were first-time fathers. With more cohabiting men reluctant to become fathers, a significantly higher proportion of the pregnancies were seen as 'unplanned' among the unmarried group. Sometimes there was a difference of opinion between the father and mother over whether the birth was 'planned' or not, and some of the cohabiting men were very unhappy throughout the pregnancy.[44] Women's ability to control their fertility and the emphasis on their exclusive right to decide if, and when, they have children or carry a pregnancy to term, may have weakened men's feelings that they are morally obliged to marry their pregnant girlfriend, as much as it has undermined taboos on pre-marital sex. Men expect uncommitted sex and, if a woman does not comply, both the man and the woman are aware that he can go elsewhere—leaving women who expect marriage and children disadvantaged.

> The accidental pregnancy has disrupted Sarah's life. Her boyfriend, who already has a broken marriage and a child, has left her and is convinced she deliberately allowed herself to become pregnant. He wants her to have an abortion, but that is not an option for Sarah. She believes that, at 26, she is ready—with the support of her family—to become a mother.[45]

A Reader's Digest/MORI poll which canvassed the opinions of men aged 16 to 25, found that only one third would commit to marriage if they were to get their girlfriend pregnant. More than a quarter said that marriage was 'not likely' and a third said it would 'depend'.[46]

When a fertile cohabiting union is converted to marriage, the parents are less likely to split up than if they continued as cohabitants, although the children are still more likely to see their parents eventually separate than those born in marriage, something which applies right across Europe.[47] In Britain, 75 per cent of couples who wed after the birth of a child were still together five years after the birth, compared with 92 per cent of the married and 48 per cent of the cohabitants.

Existing cohabitations *with children* tend to break up at four- to five-fold the rate of marriages,[48] or at 4.8 times in the British Household Panel Study.[49] Even with economic and other factors like age and duration controlled for, the odds of dissolution are at least twice as high for cohabiting couples compared to married ones. Figures for Finland show a comparable rate of break-up for cohabitations with children—five times more than the risk of experiencing divorce of children born in wedlock.[50] In the longitudinal study of children born in Christchurch, New Zealand in 1977, 43.9 per cent of those in 'de facto' unions experienced family breakdown in the first five years, compared with 10.9 per cent where the parents were legally married. Australian data on parents 18 months after the birth of a child show that 19 per cent of cohabiting couples had already separated, compared to only two per cent of married couples, or nearly a tenfold difference.[51] Even UK teenage mothers who had a child within marriage are more likely to still be wed in their thirties, compared to those who began parenthood as cohabitants—one in two compared to one in three.[52] Teenage mothers who had their first child in cohabitation had the most partners by age 33: 18 per cent had had three or more compared with five per cent of married teenage mothers and four per cent of those who had a child prior to any partnership. Those who conceived and bore a child within marriage were the least likely to be living on their own. Moreover, since cohabitations terminate sooner, as well as more frequently, than marriages, so nearly 80 per cent of the children involved were under five when their cohabiting parents parted in a recent investigation, or almost double the rate for children with formerly married parents.[53] Where parents wed after the birth of a child, work by Professor Peter McDonald from the Australian National University indicates that about 15 per cent of these marriages break up within five years, compared to 38 per cent of the relationships of continuing cohabitants[54]—or, as we saw, 25 per cent compared to 52 per cent for British fertile cohabitants in the late 1990s.[55]

Less successful cohabitants have more unstable relationships compared to those who enjoy better socio-economic conditions, just as the less materially successful among the married are particularly vulnerable to divorce. If economic circumstances worsen from one year to the other, both have 50 per cent more chance of breaking up, and conversely, 50 per cent more chance of surviving if conditions improve.[56] Overall, cohabiting parents tend to have a less successful socio-economic profile than married parents, which would tend to make their breakdown rates higher. However, the greater propensity of married parents to stay together cannot simply be 'a function of their relatively more successful circumstances',[57] as some insist, since cohabiting parents break up at much *higher rates* at similar income levels. While financial insecurity militates against personal stability, this does not account for the wide differences in dissolution rates between cohabiting and marital unions.

Chapter 3

Cohabitation And Lone-Parent Families

The Road To Lone Parenthood

Cohabitation is a route via which mothers, particularly those in relatively unfavourable economic circumstances, are 'selected' into lone parenthood. It testifies to the way in which the much lauded but ill-defined 'alternative family structures' which are supposedly replacing the conjugal two-parent family quickly devolve into the basic biological unit of mother and child. Lone parenthood via cohabitation has increased over time, more than doubling for women reaching their sixteenth birthday after 1979 and having an unwed birth before 33, compared with those who were 16 before. About 40 per cent of one-parent families are now created through the dissolution of cohabiting unions.[1] All in all, a majority of children born to cohabitants are likely to spend time with a lone parent, since only 36 per cent will live with both parents throughout childhood, compared to 70 per cent of those born to married parents.

In Scandinavia, broken cohabitations are behind the rise in single-mother families and lone parenthood, since the proportion of women both unwed and alone at the time of birth is quite low and has been relatively stable over time. In Norway, the 50 per cent of children born to unmarried mothers are mostly born into cohabitations. The family dissolution rate for ten-year-olds in 1996 when they had been born into cohabitations was between two and three times that for those born into marriage and, as elsewhere, breakdown tends to occur at a younger age. This contradicts the familiar claims about marriage and cohabitation becoming indistinguishable in Scandinavia.[2] A study of dissolution rates for 4,000 Swedish couples with one child found that, on average, cohabiting parents were three times more likely to break up than comparable married couples.[3] Again, there has been a tendency for cohabitations to become more unstable over time, as well as more likely to break up when a child is young. Where the UK differs from other countries is in the rise of solo mothers who have never been in any relationship, so that these must be added to the lone parents emerging from broken cohabitations. The 'solo' mother rate in Sweden is six per cent of all first-time mothers, ten per cent in Europe as a whole, but 15 per cent in Britain, having more than doubled since 1982.[4]

The more recent the UK birth cohort of the mothers, or the younger they are, the larger the proportion who are lone parents. Trends over time are demonstrated for children by the way in which, amongst children born in 1980, just over one in five were living within a one-parent family when they were aged 15, but this proportion was reached by age five amongst children born in 1990.

The fact that it is so short-lived is the reason why cohabitation is not replacing marriage for mothers: 'Quite quickly the couple decides either to make the commitment more permanent by formally marrying, or to dissolve the partnership'.[5] Cohabitation is an inherently unstable state. Where it is not a step leading to marriage, it is not an alternative to marriage, and there are reasons why it could not be. Kathleen Kiernan believes that:

> If cohabitation is becoming more long-standing and children are increasingly being not only born but being reared throughout their childhood in such unions, then public and private institutions will need to address the implications of this novel development.[6]

However, children are uncommonly 'reared throughout their childhood in such unions', so, in these terms, there is simply no such 'novel development'.

Cohabitation is a route via which mothers are not only 'selected' into lone parenthood, but welfare dependency. Analysis of the National Child Development Study shows how the partnership context within which teenage mothers had their first child is associated with later experiences, having implications for housing and income, as well as partnership behaviour and family building.[7] There is a greater tendency for teenage mothers who had their first child outside of marriage to be on income support in their early thirties. This was true of 27 per cent of those who gave birth as teenagers prior to any partnership, and 32 per cent of those who gave birth in a cohabiting union. The comparison is with only 14 per cent who conceived within marriage and 20 per cent with pre-marital conceptions who subsequently married. These odds of being on benefit were only marginally reduced by controls for educational attainment.

A Path Out Of Marriage

Cohabitation is not only a major route into lone parenthood. Cohabitation also delays—and, it seems, impedes and probably prevents—marriage and married parenthood. 'Partnerships', whether as marriage or cohabitation, are being generally postponed, in that 66 per cent of women born between 1963-76 entered a first partnership by the age of 24, compared with 75 per cent in the 1950-62 cohort. In turn, marriage has declined more than cohabitation has increased, so that falling numbers of marriages—or, more correctly, first marriages —have not been compensated for or fully replaced, by the rising numbers of cohabitations.[8] In the US three-quarters of the decline in the proportion of women married for the first time by age 25 was offset by increased cohabitation (and, like the UK, all of the decline in the proportion of separated and divorced persons who remarry within five years).[9] Furthermore, there is the change in the nature or meaning of cohabitation, from (usually) a prelude, or alternative, to marriage to a 'live-in' liaison, where younger people are increasingly more likely than their predecessors to end cohabitation by separation, rather than marriage.[10]

However, while partnerships are falling anyway, cohabitations are still supplanting marriages for more people over time, rather than being additional to these. The relative proportions marrying directly and cohabiting have been reversed fairly quickly in recent times, as cohabitation has become the dominant mode of first partnership. More than two-fifths of the women in the most recent birth cohort (born 1963-76) in John Ermisch's and Marco Francesconi's study had entered cohabitation by their 24th birthday, compared to one-fifth of the previous cohort, while those going directly into marriage fell—from 54 per cent to 21 per cent.[11] More than a third of first cohabiting partnerships flounder. Similarly, in the 1998 General Household Survey, 14 per cent of adults aged 16-59 reported at least one period of failed cohabitation which had not led to marriage, and nearly a quarter of those aged 25 to 34.[12] As long-term cohabitations are rare, and since cohabitations break up at a higher and faster rate than marriages, this leaves more people 'unpartnered'. After a first cohabiting partnership has dissolved, the median duration to the next partnership is five years, so that marriage is surrounded by longer periods of partnered or unpartnered singlehood over the lifetime. If recent generations of young people are not marrying, part—at least of the answer:

> ...lies in... the large proportion of persons who cohabit before any marriage, the time spent cohabiting, the relatively high risk that cohabitations dissolve and the time it takes to cohabit again. All of these contribute to a longer time before any marriage takes place and increase the chances that a person never marries.[13]

By the same token that the shift to cohabitation as a way of forging the first 'partnership' is driving the overall decline in marriage, it is behind the rise in people living alone. After the first or subsequent 'partnership' breaks down, people may not 'try again'. Moreover, while there is a benefit in terms of marital stability from delaying marriage from the teenage years to the early twenties, there seem to be no additional benefits from further delaying marriage to the late twenties or thirties: the opposite could be the case. As such, 'partnership turnover' itself is not extensive, even if single, divorced, separated and cohabiting people are more likely than the married to have had a previous period of cohabitation that did not lead to marriage.[14] Data from the European Family and Fertility Surveys show how the majority of British women aged 35-39 have only had one partnership, whether marriage or cohabitation. Around 20 per cent have two, and five per cent have had three or more—close to Sweden's six per cent. (This does not, of course, register intimate non-co-residential partnerships.)[15]

Not only the delay in first partnership, but substitution of cohabitation for direct marriage is also implicated in the postponement of—and possible relinquishment of—motherhood. The rise in maternal age and fall in the birthrate is accounted for by the decline in marital births, although a majority of births still occur in marriage rather than outside.

Does Cohabitation Prevent Divorce?

However, should the higher rates of instability for cohabitations—especially those without children—be considered at all surprising, let alone of any concern? After all, is it not the task of cohabitation to weed out mismatches, or potentially incompatible mates, by testing out the relationship? Surely, cohabitation as a preparation for marriage or 'probationary period' is more likely to ensure that those couples who do survive and eventually marry are more likely to have successful and lasting marriages? As divorce increased, its possibility has worried people, particularly as many of the negative consequences, such as economic deprivation and the painful disruption of personal ties, became widely known. The upward climb in the risk of divorce seems to underline the need to have a 'trial run' in an attempt to reduce mismatches or unsuccessful marriages, with all their legal implications. From here they could assess or evaluate the quality and possible future of their relationships, with the less propitious terminated without all the problems of divorce. For others, the cohabiting period could be the time to strengthen interpersonal relationships without the responsibilities of children—relationships which might later become marriages with enhanced chances of stability.[16] Hence, since the more problematic unions would have been cleared away and the more positive enhanced, the quality of marriages would be raised as much as the likelihood of divorce reduced.

A further implication is that surviving cohabitations should be at least as, if not more, successful and happy than marriages, since—as is often claimed—the people are together 'because they want to be, not because they have to be'.

Unfortunately, the expectation of a positive relationship between cohabitation and marital stability 'has been shattered in recent years'. While 'studies are consistent with expectations of high dissolution rates among cohabitants before marriage, they provide no evidence that cohabitation experience leads to lower rates of dissolution after marriage'.[17] Instead, the argument has become one of whether or not marriages preceded by cohabitation are less stable and have a higher chance of breaking down than those not preceded by cohabitation. Research findings published by John Haskey in 1992 reported that UK couples marrying in 1970-74 were 30 per cent more likely to divorce after five years if they had cohabited; those marrying in 1975-79 were 40 per cent more likely, and those marrying in 1980-84 were 50 per cent more likely. Allowing for extra time living together, previously cohabiting couples still seemed 20 per cent more likely to divorce after 15 years of marriage.[18] The Australian Family Formation Project found that, after five years of marriage, 13 per cent of those who had cohabited would divorce compared to six per cent of those who had not cohabited. Ten years later, the proportions were 26 to 14 per cent. After 20 years, it was 56 compared to 27 per cent.[19] In Canada, pre-marital cohabitants also have over twice the risk of divorce in any year of marriage compared to non-cohabitants.[20] Not only has cohabitation prior to marriage seemed positively associated with the perceived likelihood of dissolution of the current marriage, but the longer the cohabitation before marriage, the greater, it seemed, was the likelihood of divorce.[21]

However, some studies indicate that the odds of dissolution for those who have only cohabited with their future spouse are no greater than for those who marry directly, as with the National Child Development Study in the UK, where the risk of a first partnership ending before 33 was similar for those who had cohabited before marriage compared with those who had not.[22] In the European Family and Fertility Studies,[23] marriages preceded by cohabitation were almost as likely to survive to ten years from the start of the partnership as those not preceded by cohabitation. When John Haskey added a set of questions to the Omnibus Survey, carried out by the Office for National Statistics on a monthly basis, which asked about cohabiting relationships which had ended prior to the current marriage/cohabitation, it allowed for a comparison between the probability of divorce for those who had married without cohabiting, and those who had cohabited only with their future spouse.[24] There was no significant difference, which suggests that the association found in other studies between pre-marital cohabitation and divorce might be due to those who have experienced 'partnership turnover'—or multiple cohabitations—before marriage. Unfortunately, cohabitants are more likely to have had a succession of 'partnerships', compared to the married.

US research shows contradictory results. Some researchers have found that, when marital duration was counted from the beginning of the co-residential union, only those who cohabited more than once prior to marriage had higher odds of dissolution.[25] Others, using the National Survey of Families and Households, found that the impact of cohabitation on later marital disruption remained positive and significant, even if this was only with the future spouse.[26] None of this alters the fact that legal unions are more stable than cohabitations, independently of how they began.

Moreover, even where little difference is found in the risk of break-down in first partnerships amongst cohabitants who subsequently married and those couples who married directly, this does not hold where fertile unions are considered. Those who marry after the birth of their first child have been found to be at a particularly high risk of divorce in Australia, Britain, Canada, Sweden and the US, although there is little difference in break-up by five in Sweden, Norway, Austria and West Germany shown in the European Fertility and Family Surveys.[27] Ninety-two per cent of marital unions survive to five years after the birth of a child in Great Britain; those who have cohabited and then married show a 75 per cent survival rate, and those who cohabit only show a 48 per cent survival rate. From other research we find that, with other factors held constant, around 20 per cent of women born in 1958 who experienced their first birth prior to marriage underwent marital dissolution within eight years, whereas the figure is 13 per cent of those who delayed their childbearing a couple of years after marriage.[28]

If a marriage is more likely to break down when one or both partners have had a previous cohabiting relationship so, it seems, is a second or subsequent relationship where the partner(s) have come from a cohabitation rather than a marriage. In the DSS longitudinal sample of lone parents, around 38 per cent of ex-cohabitants left lone parent-hood between 1991 and 1995, but more than a third of those who had found new partners separated again. However, lone parents who had been divorced, separated from marriage or who had never previously lived with a 'partner' were more likely to stay in a new relationship.[29]

Very many children in unmarried-couple households are born not in the present union, but in a previous union of one of the partners, usually the mother. While many parents who leave marriages or cohabitations form 'reconstituted' or 'blended' families through a further marriage or cohabitation, these unions are particularly unstable, with one New Zealand study revealing that only about a third will last five years.[30]

Such findings still indicate that—at very least—cohabitation does nothing to strengthen marriage and that, in some conditions, pre-marital cohabitation is associated with increased risk of marital breakdown. Kathleen Kiernan surmises that: 'Pre-marital cohabitations may be an effective way of selecting out partnerships with an enhanced risk of breakdown [since] the most fragile partnerships were cohabiting unions that had not converted into marriage'.[31] If this were so, marriages preceded by cohabitation would be stronger and there would be more surviving marriages when, in reality, this is not so. It also suggests that people who experience a broken cohabitation, and then go on to marry another partner, might then have more stable marriages, because they have 'learnt' from the previous experience or have escaped from an unpropitious relationship. In practice, the opposite is the case, since the second relationship stands a greater chance of breaking down.

Committed To Parenthood, If Not Partners?

If cohabitations with children are much more fragile than marriages, does the parent/child bond nevertheless persist equally and irrespective of whether it is made in informal or formal relationships? After all, the way forward is now seen to lie in the separation of adult/adult ties from parent/child ties, in the belief that the latter are, or can easily be made to be, more enduring, irrespective of the type of relationship in which they originate.

However, marriage seems to engender a 'higher degree of investment in the parental relationship', than is the case with cohabitants and never-together couples, and this outlasts the union. Mavis Maclean and John Eekelaar found that formerly married fathers in the UK provide income transfers to the mother of their children in 68 per cent of cases (where she had not remarried or begun cohabiting with another man), or at more than double the rate, of former cohabitants or men who had never lived with the mother (who paid at only 32 and 31 per cent). Regular support was paid by 44 per cent of the formerly married, compared to only 26 per cent of the 'never-together' fathers and 16 per cent of the former cohabitants. Only ten per cent of formerly married fathers in full-time work and living on their own paid nothing, compared to nearly a third of former cohabitants and never-together men in the same circumstances. Much the same was true of continued, committed contact with the children.[32] This was despite the way in which married fathers had more incentives to break with the children (where, for example, they had made other relationships). The researchers have tried to attribute this to the longer time that married fathers had lived with the children, and so got to know them more, even though this, in itself, resulted from the earlier breakdown of cohabitations.

As it is, the untoward results replicate the findings of Judith A. Seltzer on the father's role after separation, using the US National Survey of Families and Households. Nearly a half of the mothers' reports were from women who had never married the children's fathers and nearly 40 per cent of these men had no social involvement with their children in the past year, compared to just over 18 per cent where the parents had been married. Underscoring other US research, only 28.5 per cent had paid any child support, compared to over 64 per cent of the married fathers, and when they did it was under a half of the value of that paid where the parents had been married.[33]

A similar pattern is present in Scandinavia, where fathers have lower rates of contact with children produced in cohabitations, compared to those born within marriage, when the union breaks down.[34] Marriage strengthens the children's claim to the economic resources and social capital of both their parents—even when it has ended.

Chapter 4

Troubled Relationships

Better Relationships?

As well as being as or more divorce-prone than marriages without previous cohabitation experience, there is some evidence that marriages preceded by cohabitation also show lower levels of commitment, tend to be significantly lower on measures of marital quality, and have higher levels of disagreement and instability.[1] It is marriages preceded by long cohabitations (i.e. two years or more) which seem to be particularly characterised by low marital quality as well as having a higher perceived likelihood of divorce.[2] For Australia, Sarantakos found that the proportion of those reporting low or very low levels of satisfaction was three times larger among couples with pre-marital cohabitation (36 per cent) than among couples without (12 per cent). It was the couples with one or more spouses involved in multiple pre-marital cohabitation experience who more often had low marital quality than couples with single or no pre-marital cohabital experience.[3] The same applied to low levels of happiness and both high and long-lasting levels of conflict. The more cohabital encounters, the more frequent and the more serious were the conflicts. Again, this casts doubt on the hopes for pre-marital cohabitation as a means of ensuring the compatibility of prospective spouses, and building the interpersonal skills important to successful marriage.

A picture of more troubled and less satisfying or successful relationships is also pronounced and consistent for surviving cohabitations compared to existing marriages so that, while the evidence provides about the most emphatic rejection possible of any notion that cohabitations are as stable as marriages, it also suggests that such relationships are often not as significant or synonymous in other respects. Compared with the married in the US National Survey of Families and Households, cohabitants were almost twice as likely to report that they felt that their relationship was in trouble over the past year, after age differences and duration were taken into account.[4] Similarly, Sarantakos' Australian cohabitants were more likely to report conflicts than the married, at 29 compared to 18 per cent.[5] Paul R. Amato's and Alan Booth's Study of Marital Instability Over the Life Course followed the marital careers of over two thousand married people and assessed the long-term impact of family life on children who had lived with their interviewed parents in 1980 and had reached majority by 1992.[6] While reporting that cohabiting and married offspring did not seem to differ in their reported happiness or interaction, relationship problems and instability were dramatically higher among cohabiting than married individuals.

Significantly, in Susan MacRae's sample of long-term cohabiting mothers, only one in two would choose the same partner if given a second chance in life. This compares to three-quarters of mothers who married after or before having the baby and nearly 80 per cent of married mothers who never cohabited.[7] A 1996 analysis of the National Child Development Study rated happiness in relationships with partners according to a scale. The least happy were the never-married cohabiting women and, in all categories, the cohabitants rated their relationship less happy than did married respondents.[8] A similar US comparison of the relationship quality of married and cohabiting couples of less than ten years duration concluded that cohabitants were less happy with their relationships as well as less committed to these than the married.[9]

Relationships of long duration are specifically implicated in reports of the poor quality of cohabitational unions in the US.[10] These are precisely the relationships where there are likely to be no marriage plans and constitute—if any do—the 'alternative' to marriage. The same is reported for Australia: if cohabitation was defined, explicitly or not, by the cohabitants as a step to marriage or as an informal engagement, the proportion of couples reporting successful relationships was large —but where it was defined as an alternative to marriage, the proportion was small.[11] Couples without marriage plans increase as a proportion of cohabitants as cohabitation duration increases, as those with plans are more likely to be selected out through marriage. In turn, those who have had previously disrupted cohabitations or marriages are more likely not to plan marriage than those without. This might reflect a relative absence of skills to sustain lasting, intimate relationships. Using data from the 1987-1988 National Survey of Families and Households, Susan L. Brown and Alan Booth evaluated the extent to which cohabitation was similar to marriage for black and white Americans aged 19-48. Controlling for relationship duration and demographic characteristics of their subjects, they reported the now familiar finding that cohabitants, on average, have poorer quality relationships than their married counterparts. Moreover, those who reported plans to marry their partners were involved in unions that were far closer to those of the married in quality than cohabitants without definite plans to marry. The relationship quality of the married and the cohabitants with plans to marry were affected in the same way by the presence of biological children, and similar results applied where there were children from previous unions. Much the same was found for Australia, where spouses who saw cohabitation as a temporary stopgap until marriage was practicable were found in a higher proportion among those who reported more positive life experience and higher marital quality than those who perceived cohabitation as an alternative to marriage, but later decided to marry.[12]

It might be objected that plans to marry are affected by the relationship quality, or emerge from this, rather than vice versa. This turned out not to be the case in Susan L. Brown's and Alan Booth's analysis from the National Survey of Families and Households; rather it was marriage plans that seemed to affect relationship quality for the better. (Again, this undermines notions that marriage best emerges from a 'trial' to test out compatibility.) Mate selection is an aspect of this, as seen in Sarantakos' Australian study, where cohabitants who originally chose their partner as a 'friend' or a 'flatmate', or even 'just a cohabitant' and who subsequently married that person were found in higher proportions among those reporting low levels of marital quality, than those who choose their partner as a future spouse or life-long companion. It seems that cohabitation can only be another form of marriage if it leads to marriage—by prior intent![13]

Domestic Violence And Cohabitation

While Brown and Booth found that US cohabitants experienced more disagreement than their married counterparts, had lower levels of happiness and fairness, then they also reported more fights or violence.[14] In Carol Smart's and Pippa Stevens' in-depth study, violence and sexual infidelity were the two most commonly occurring reasons given by the 20 women as to why the cohabitation broke down.[15]

These findings are part of pervasive indications that domestic violence is higher among cohabitants than it is among the married. The US crime victimisation rate for two decades up to 1992 shows how violent crime per 1,000 females aged 12 or older was 43 for unmarried women, 45 for divorced and separated women and 11 for married women.[16] In turn, only 29 per cent of the violent crime towards women committed by intimates involved a current spouse, while 42 per cent involved boyfriends or partners and another 12 per cent an ex-spouse.[17] Drawing on a study of 13,000 adults assessed periodically between 1987 and 1993, Nadine F. Marks and James D. Lambert found that 'moderate domestic violence', or hitting, pushing or throwing objects at a partner, was half as frequent with married couples or cohabiting couples planning to marry, than it was with cohabiting couples who were not planning to marry.[18]

Marital status was the strongest predictor of abuse—ahead of race, age, education or housing conditions—to emerge from data examined by an agency of the US Department of Health and Human Services in 1994. This revealed how unmarried women were three to four times more likely to be physically abused by their boyfriends while pregnant than married women by their husbands.[19] Confirming earlier findings, the US National Family Violence Resurvey showed that almost 35 out of every 100 cohabiting couples experienced a physical assault during the previous year, compared to 15 per 100 married couples and 20 per 100 dating couples. Moreover, cohabiting couples had the highest rates for each of the three specific types of violence, involving women only, men only and both partners. For example, in 18 out of every 100 cohabiting couples, both were violent, double the rate for dating and married couples. For minor violence committed by both partners, cohabiting couples had roughly double the rate of other groups, and six times the rate of severe violence committed by both partners. Marital status effects on violence were the same for every age group. White collar rates of violence were lower than blue collar rates, and the difference between married and cohabiting couples was somewhat less pronounced among white collar couples than blue collar couples but, even after controlling for education and occupation, the marital status difference in assault rates remained, for male and female violence and both for minor and severe violence.

A similar situation seems to be present in New Zealand statistics for protection and non-molestation orders under the Domestic Violence Act 1992. While 96 per cent of the orders have been granted against men, only 35 per cent have involved husbands compared with the 50 per cent involving *de facto* partners. Even given that the *de facto* partner figure includes men in same sex or other 'close relationships' categories, and even allowing for hypothetical differences in action women may take against cohabitants, but not husbands, the difference between the two groups is considerable.[20] A similar picture is presented by a study of 234 American men charged with domestic violence. The most frequently cited relationship was cohabitation (48 per cent), the second was divorced or separated (27 per cent). Only 19 men were married spouses.[21]

The British Crime Survey of England and Wales for 1997[22] shows that while the average chance of experiencing violence in the year was 4.7 per cent, young men aged 16 to 24 were most at risk, at 20.9 per cent, followed by lone parents, at 11.9 per cent. The proportion of adults who were victims of violence as a result of their living arrangements was only 2.7 per cent of the married, compared to 6.4 per cent of cohabitants, 8.4 per cent of the separated, 6.0 per cent of the divorced and 11.3 per cent of the single. The 'high overall risk of violence among lone parents' is 'solely because they are far more likely to be victims of domestic violence'. Their risk of experiencing other types of violence is similar to that of other adults under 60. Moreover, 42 per cent of single-parent households reported being victimised more than once in 1997, higher than rates for low income, social renters, private renters, or people living in areas of high physical disorder (33.5 per cent). Of the 11.9 per cent of lone parents reporting violence, 6.9 per cent was domestic, and another three per cent from an acquaintance.

According to influential feminist analysis, wife beating is a reflection of patriarchal norms, which support male dominance in marriage, where 'marriage is the mechanism by which the patriarchy is maintained'.[23] Prominent scholars of family violence have, accordingly, referred to 'the marriage license as a hitting license', or something that permits or encourages men to abuse their wives.[24] Therefore, with less marriage, and more 'consensual unions' there should be less 'wife-beating'. However, since subsequent investigations have revealed that physical assaults may be more common and more severe among cohabiting couples, and given that cohabitation as an alternative living arrangement has steadily increased since 1970, 'more individuals may be at risk not only of minor violence, but severe violence'.[25] Significantly, couples with multiple cohabitational experience seem to be particularly prone to report violence.[26]

This is evident in the work of Geoff Dench, which records the prevalence and advance of 'alternative' family perspectives amongst different ethnic groups in London. Supposedly, African Caribbeans have a high regard for lone-parent families and consensual unions—an idea 'partly grounded in sexual politics originating among white people' who have conscripted Afro-Caribbeans as their champions.[27] However, the values and behaviour attributed to this group are held mainly by those who grew up in Britain where, among younger Afro-Caribbeans, there is the strongest rejection of conventional family life and adoption of 'alternative' values emphasising choice and the optional nature of family roles, compared to other ethnic groups in the UK, and migrants who grew up in the Caribbean. This is accompanied by the most far reaching adoption of alternative lifestyles in terms of the lowest marriage, highest unwed birth and lone parenthood rates, and a level of lone-adult households running at 56 per cent compared to 22 per cent for those born in the Caribbean, and 25 per cent for white British, despite far more older people in the last two groups. Also present was the highest incidence of reported sexual conflict and sexual polarisation, as well as marginalisation of men, who were highly likely to be unproductive (47 per cent were unemployed), apathetic and generally peripheral to community affairs.

Explaining why the US National Survey of Families and Households confirmed how nearly three times as many cohabitants admitted to hitting, shoving or throwing things at their partner in the past year compared to the married (14 to five per cent), Jan E. Stets found that cohabitants tend to be younger, less likely to have ties to groups and organisations, less bound to their relationships, more likely to be depressed and to have alcohol problems.[28]

It is possible that kin and friends may put fewer constraints on how cohabitants act where, instead of encouraging them to fulfil certain expectations (involved, for example, in a legal marriage), they leave them freer to lead their own lives. More, they may also distance or disassociate themselves and be unprepared to lend material and other support, or otherwise invest in, relationships which appear to have no recognised place or potential in the network of kin ties. Such reactions are consistent with the cohabiting lifestyle, which implies that the individuals somehow set or make up their own standards, rather than being guided by the rules of society. Moreover, cohabitants may guard against being tied to partners or participating in organisations as these involve being subject to others' expectations and possible restrictions, which are threatening to the freedoms they enjoy. However, these may not be the only factors influencing aggressive behaviour. The very nature of being in a less committed relationship may create its own dynamics. Elsewhere, cohabiting men have been found to be more tolerant of rape.[29] In Australia, Sarantakos found that not only were there more cases of violence, including violence lasting several years, among cohabiting couples and those with pre-marital cohabital experience, compared to married couples without cohabital experience, but more couples with cohabital experience tolerated and justified violence than couples without such experience.[30]

Health And Cohabitation

Cohabitation is not only more likely to be more unstable and troubled than marriage, but it does not seem to confer the same advantages as marriage in terms of, for example, the health of men and women. There is now 'conclusive evidence to show that marriage is a "healthy environment" associated with lower mortality and morbidity',[31] which has 'now reached the status of a truism... consistently appearing in all studies where it is measured'.[32] Compared to the general population, divorced and widowed men are now more than twice as likely to consult their doctors for mental disorders and divorced/ widowed women are one-and-a-half times as likely. This difference is magnified for all treatments for psychiatric illness, where the admission rate to psychiatric units or hospitals at times approaches tenfold for the divorced compared to married individuals.[33] Swedish figures show that there is a fourfold higher risk of divorced men acquiring a psychiatric record, compared to comparable married men and a 2.5 higher risk for divorced women.[34]

In England and Wales, single and widowed men have roughly double the death rates of the married at all ages, and the odds for divorced men are increased by more than a half.[35] It is in line with an age-specific death rate for divorced people in the US, which is 84 per cent higher than for married people, and there are similar findings in Australia.[36] Cohabitation with another adult does not appear to protect men or women from much of the increased mortality risk that accompanies singleness.[37] Such living arrangements have a modest effect on the risk of dying for single and divorced people.

It could be argued that the selection of healthy people into marriage, and a rejection of the unhealthy by divorce accounts for differences in mortality, sickness and survival. Those with the most to offer a potential mate marry, those with somewhat less to offer cohabit, and those with the least remain single and live alone.[38] In contrast to social causation arguments, where living conditions precede and predict health, selection arguments posit that individuals' characteristics influence the likelihood of entering into different types of relationships or statuses. Thus, marriage simply identifies healthy people, not only through the direct exclusion of the mentally and physically ill, but also through a wide range of criteria including income, appearance, family background, risk-taking behaviour, health-related habits and emotional stability.[39] An obvious example involves alcoholism, where heavy drinkers are less marriageable and twice as many marriages complicated by alcoholism end in divorce compared to ones without alcohol problems.[40]

Selection is certainly at play, and in a more complex way than usually imagined,[41] but it would be doing a big injustice to the evidence not to attribute to marriage some, or even a large part, of the better outcomes. The US Panel Study of Income Dynamics followed 11,112 individuals over a 17 year period.[42] Marriage resulted in an immediate and substantial reduction in the risk of dying for men—consistent with either more risk behaviour in single men and/or the selection of those with the best physical and mental health into marriage. However, for both sexes, the hazards of dying also fell significantly with marital duration, suggesting a cumulation of benefits over time, with the decrease significantly larger for women.

Like those between the married and the single, differences in health outcomes for the married and cohabiting are likely owed to differences in behaviour which, in turn, may be related to the nature of the cohabiting relationship and the people this attracts. The unmarried are more likely to have negative health behaviours, or to smoke and drink heavily and be substance abusers, to take risks and be less likely to have an orderly lifestyle.[43] The greater the behavioural component in the aetiology of death, the greater the gap in mortality between the married and the maritally disrupted or uninvolved. Marriage provides someone who monitors a person's well-being and health-related behaviour and encourages self-regulation, something seen in the positive effects of marriage on health behaviours in elderly as well as younger people.[44] Affiliation and obligations to others also inhibit risky behaviours. Marriage gives people structure in their lives, or a framework for decision-making and sense of meaning; helping to develop and maintain a coherent set of norms, values, expectations, and guidelines for action.[45] Such protection, like selection, is particularly important for men. Wives exert a positive influence on their husbands' smoking, drinking[46] and eating habits, encourage them to go for health checks and do much to provide a settled and organised home life. In contrast, Sotirios Sarantakos in *Living Together in Australia*[47] describes how 'cohabitants, especially women, seem to tolerate in their partner types of behaviour which marriers consider unacceptable. Drugs, drinking, social deviance and sexual freedom are often accepted more in a cohabitation environment than in a marriage environment'.

Cohabitation represents freedom from the demands of marriage, which is why it has been part of the toleration or assumption of 'alternative' beliefs and practices, so cohabitants do not derive the same mental health benefits from their relationships as married people do from their marriages. In the US, the Rutgers Health and Human Development Project, using a longitudinal sample of otherwise comparable cohabitants, married and single people, found that the cohabitants did not differ from the never-married in terms of mental health.[48] Cohabitants reported significantly more depression and nearly three times more alcohol problems than the married; indeed, their alcohol problems were the highest of all groups. Even controlling for pre-marital or pre-cohabitation levels of problems and unconventionality, as well as many other factors, cohabitation was a strong predictor of alcohol problems, particularly for men. Indeed, while those who married during the seven-year research period halved any pre-existing problem, and singles cut it by a quarter, there was no reduction over time for cohabitants. In turn, there were no differences in levels of alcohol problems or depression between married people who did, and did not, cohabit before marriage. Thus, it seems that: 'cohabiting relationships are associated with lifestyles that include problem drinking and that a commitment to conventionality is made only after marriage. Likewise, the role of spouses, especially wives, in exerting social control over behaviours like problem drinking, arises only after marriage, not during cohabitation'.[49]

Moreover, the currently married have turned out to be consistently better off than any other group on measures of happiness and life satisfaction[50] in analyses of the relationship between marital status and psychological well-being in 19 countries. Whatever their income or education, married people report greater happiness and less depression than cohabitants, who report greater well-being than those who live without another adult.[51] For the US, annual rates of depression among cohabiting couples are among three times what they are among married couples.[52] In providing a primary relationship as a buffer against the stresses of everyday life and support in its vicissitudes, marriage is the archetypal source of all three forms of social support—emotional, cognitive, and material—even if, for some individuals, it may be more a source of stress.[53] Marriage connects people not only to another individual, but to networks of exchange and support with entitled access to group resources and assistance. At the same time, all this provides married people with higher levels of social integration. Significantly, while the Advisory Board on Family Law still believed in 1998/9 that a 'formal commitment to family life' can exist apart from marriage, it nevertheless emphasised that 'it should be recognised that there are positive socio-economic benefits in marriage, in addition to its value in providing stability for children'.[54]

As Good As Married, Or Same As Single?

Cohabitation differs from marriage not only in terms of relative stability, satisfaction, health outcomes, and acceptance of parental responsibility. As we have already seen, such distinctions are often related to differences in behaviour during the 'living in' period for cohabitants compared to the married. Cohabitants, especially male cohabitants, have economic, social and sexual behaviour patterns that are more like those of single than married people. If married men spend significantly more time in the labour market than single men, then male cohabitants with children have rates of economic inactivity that resemble single and divorced men. A third aged between 25 and 39 were unemployed or otherwise out of the labour market in the British Household Panel Study, compared with 14 per cent of married men with children.[55] Men in more precarious economic positions are, of course, less likely to marry, and cohabiting men with children tend also to be less well qualified and educated. However, as already mentioned, this may not be the whole, or even the major, part of the story, since the 'marriage premium' or tendency for married men to earn more than single men by being more productive and successful at work has been found to be missing or far lower for cohabiting men.[56] While male marriageability depends on employment and income, and men who are unable to support families find marriage less attractive, marriage itself clearly promotes male labour market involvement and success.

Such differences as have been found in performance between single and married men cannot be explained in terms of location, union membership, labour market experience, number of dependents, occupation or education.[57] Significantly, in Sarantakos' Australian study, the perception of work was more positive among the married than among cohabitants. Unemployed marrieds were also more likely than unemployed cohabitants to accept unconditionally any type of work. In general, unskilled and unemployed young cohabitants were more likely to be against work as a value, and to see leisure as more significant in providing 'personal fulfilment and gratification'.[58]

Similarly with sexual behaviour, only 43 per cent of cohabiting men in the UK reported being faithful to their partners in a five-year period, compared with nearly 90 per cent of married men.[59] Indeed, 24 per cent reported running two or more relationships at the same time. When comparing the number of sexual relationships in the previous year, only 4.5 per cent of married men reported two or more partners, compared to 15 per cent of men in a cohabiting relationship. Although the proportion with serial monogamy will be influenced by the shorter duration of cohabiting relationships, the high numbers with concurrent relationships suggest that cohabitation is more loosely linked with fidelity. Data from a US survey of 1,235 women in relationships in 1991, show how 20 per cent of the cohabiting women cheated on their partners, as opposed to only four per cent of the married women.[60]

> The influence of living with a partner as a measure of commitment is unclear, since those who are cohabiting show patterns that are more similar to those who are single, divorced or separated than to those who are married.[61]

While there might have been a general increase in children born to the unmarried, and while this may be linked to more widespread cohabitation, cohabiting women have much lower fertility than comparable married women. Larger numbers and proportions of non-marital births primarily reflect increased exposure to risk through the rising incidence of cohabitation, which is nonetheless accompanied by a higher rejection of parenthood by cohabitants compared to married people. Abortions are around four times more frequent with pregnancies involving cohabiting rather than married women.[62] In Sotirios Sarantakos' Australian study, 38 per cent of cohabitants had children living with them, but only 29 per cent of these were born into the cohabiting unions. Most belonged to previous marriages or relationships. None of those who had children had planned to do so. Abortion appeared to be commonly used, suggesting that 'cohabitants attempt to avoid childbirth at all costs'.[63]

Those who intend to remain childless seem to be more likely to cohabit. For one US sample, the percentage of cohabitants intending to have a child in the next two years was almost 40 per cent lower than for the married as, on this as in other important issues, cohabitants are closer to single than married people.[64] The picture is similar for New Zealand, where cohabiting couples are less likely to have children, or 40 per cent compared to the 57 per cent of married couples. Cohabiting couples also have fewer children than married couples. Almost half (46 per cent) have only one child, compared with a third of married couples, who are also more likely to have three or more children. The pattern is similar for the over-40s, where there are many older divorcees. This cannot be explained by the younger age profile of cohabiting couples, although the fact that cohabitants are in the younger age groups appears to be an important reason why more are likely to have a child under five than married couples.

Not only do cohabitants, especially male cohabitants, have economic, social and sexual behaviour patterns that are more like those of single than married people, they clearly have attitudes to match. The insistence of fathers that they continue to behave like single men without responsibilities emerges as a prominent reason why cohabitations involving children collapse without being converted to marriage. As one mother commented in Carol Smart's and Pippa Stevens' study: 'He carried on as he would have done, and regardless of whether the children were there or not. He was the third child so, if anything, life's easier for me now [we're separated]'. Interviews with the men provided the other side of the coin. Where the women spoke of the father as refusing to take his responsibilities seriously and settling down, the men spoke of feeling trapped by domesticity. While the women spoke of violence as a major reason for giving up on the relationship, the men identified criminal behaviour, taking or dealing in illegal drugs and drinking problems.[65]

Chapter 5

The Outcomes For Children

Overwhelmingly, research to date on cohabitation deals with outcomes for the couples involved, there being a paucity of evidence when it comes to comparing outcomes for the children of cohabiting, compared to married or lone parents, and that which exists is largely oblique. We know that, for example, the infant mortality rate for babies registered by the mother alone, or by both parents from different addresses, is between 45 to 68 per cent higher than that for babies born inside marriage, but still 25 to 35 per cent higher for infants whose births were registered by the unwed parents from the same address.[1]

Many children in unmarried-couple households were born in a previous union. Neglect and abuse is particularly associated with the presence of new 'partners' of the mother. Step-fathers, or 'live-in' and visiting boyfriends, constitute the most powerful risk factor for child maltreatment, being hugely over represented as perpetrators of severe physical abuse, sexual abuse and child killing.[2] The behaviour of the mother is also affected by the presence of new 'partners': those mothers living with a 'partner' after divorce were reported as more aggressive than those living with the father in a study of adolescents from comprehensive schools in South Wales.[3] If the most safe family environment is one where both biological parents are married to each other, then the most unsafe of all family environments is where the mother is living with someone who has neither a biological or legal tie to her child. Most abuse-prevalence studies look at step-parent families (married and unmarried) in comparison with intact families. One study that looked at the relationship between child abuse and the marital background of the parents found that the rate of severe abuse was 14 times higher than in a biological married family for a child living alone with a biological mother, 20 times more likely where the child was living with cohabiting biological parents and 33 times higher where the mother was cohabiting with a man who was not the biological father.[4]

Family disruption is driving the recent marked rise in youth homelessness which has fundamentally altered the nature of the homeless population, with a major change in the circumstances in which youngsters now leave home.[5] This used to be to find work, but now it is likely to be the 're-marriage or re-partnering of their own parents', with abuse from step-fathers, or abandonment, abuse and neglect from mothers with boyfriends, pushing them out of the house.

When mothers remarry or cohabit, the quality of parenting is still likely to be lower than in families with two biological parents. A new adult often means more disruption for the child. Step-fathers are less likely to be committed to the child's welfare than biological fathers, and are less likely to serve as a check on the mother's behaviour. Rather than assisting with the responsibilities of parenting, step-fathers may compete with the child for the mother's time, adding to the mother's and the child's level of stress. Even when a step-father tries to play an active role his efforts may be rejected or undermined by the mother because she does not trust his judgement. In cohabiting unions, issues of authority and trust are described as even more problematic by Sara McLanahan, and G. Sandefur, in their analysis of the effects on children of growing up in different family settings. In the National Survey of Families and Households, remarried and cohabiting mothers were the least involved with their children. They shared fewer meals, they read to their children less often, and they participated in fewer outside activities. Supervision falls: while 28 per cent of remarried mothers reported never leaving their child alone, this compared to 20 per cent with a 'partner'.[6] US research indicates that children in families with their mother and her cohabiting partner have lower academic performance, lower initiative, and more school problems than children from families with two continuously married parents, after controlling for economic resources, socio-demographic characteristics and parental behaviour.

Again, considering the high break-up rate of cohabitations and the prevalence of cohabitation after divorce or parental separation, more children in cohabiting households are likely to have experienced previous family disruption as, by the same token, more children of married couples are likely to be with their two original parents. This is certainly the case with Sotirios Sarantakos' longitudinal Australian cohabitation study. This involved 330 cohabiting and 330 married units, matched on a number of criteria, like age, socio-economic status, educational level, other personal attributes and relationship duration. Stage three of his investigations, conducted in the 1990s, focused primarily on children's issues, such as educational and social outcomes, quality of life, substance abuse and delinquency. One study used sub-sets of a total of 174 children living in married-couple families, with heterosexual cohabitants and with homosexual cohabitants (predominantly lesbian) recruited from another project on homosexual couples.[7] In this school-based investigation, children of married couples were significantly more likely to do well at school, in academic and social terms, than those of cohabiting heterosexual and homosexual couples, and marriage seemed to provide the best environment for development, in being 'more positive, supportive, rich, rewarding, secure and guiding'.[8] The children of the married couples achieved the highest scores in educational assessment and the children of the homosexual couples the lowest, this being most pronounced for language in the areas of verbal and composition skills. Mathematical ability in children of homosexual cohabitants was below the average scores for all students and well below that for the children of heterosexual cohabitants and married couples. Only in social studies were the three groups roughly commensurate. Insofar as personal adjustment was assessed, the sociability scores for the children of homosexual couples were well below those of the two other groups, with the children of married couples doing best, where (as seen) relationships with peers tended to be particularly poor. Married parents controlled and directed their children more than the couples of the other two groups, where children of homosexual cohabitants enjoyed the greatest autonomy, followed by children of cohabiting heterosexual couples.

However, it seems reasonable to assume that parental divorce or separation and step-parenthood have important roles in explaining the difference in educational development of the children in the three contexts. Many children of heterosexual cohabitants had experienced divorce, as had those of homosexual cohabitants, where all of the children were born in a previous relationship. In the latter, the family situation reflects the 'step-parent factor' in the most vivid and exaggerated way. With married couples and, to a lesser extent, cohabiting heterosexual couples, both parents were likely to be involved with the child's education. With most homosexual couples, only the natural parent of the child provided assistance, personal support and interest in their school work, as well as carrying responsibility for the control of the child. Exemplifying the situation found elsewhere in step-relationships, where the natural parent tends to have less interest and investment in their child compared with biological parents in original families, it was far more common for homosexual parents to have no firm expectations concerning the education and future of their child. There was an obvious trend among the children of both homosexual and heterosexual cohabitants to leave school and home as early as possible and set up on their own.

The delinquency aspect of Sarantakos' work dealt with 512 older children (aged 11 upwards) who had been present at the beginning of the study. Three hundred and forty eight were 'common' children in being related by blood to both parents, and 164 were related by blood to one parent only. Nearly three-quarters of the children who committed criminal offences were those of cohabiting couples and just over one-quarter were children of married couples. Moreover, the average number of reported offences committed by children of married couples was 1.21, while that of cohabiting couples was 1.73. These findings overlapped with the way in which significantly more offenders came from broken, compared to stable homes. While 28 per cent of the children from broken homes committed an offence, only eight per cent of those from stable homes did so. In turn, the results—as in much other research—showed how lack of or low levels of family cohesion were associated with delinquency, as was hostility at home, with most delinquents perceiving their parents as hostile, rather than loving and caring. There were significantly more non-offenders coming from non-violent families than violent families, and offenders were more likely to have indifferent, rather than interested, parents. These factors related to the quality of the family environment regardless of whether the parents were married or lived together, but the high frequency of delinquents among children of cohabiting couples was the result of a higher frequency of interpersonal problems in the lifestyle of cohabiting parents.[9] Similar considerations apply to further findings that significantly more children of cohabiting, compared to married, couples seem to have been less successful in the area of employment. Children of cohabiting couples also appear in larger proportions than children of married couples among those who have used illicit drugs, begun drinking earlier in life and drink more.[10]

A survey into the mental health of children and adolescents in Great Britain, carried out on behalf of the Department of Health, found that children living with cohabiting couples were 50 per cent more likely to have a mental health problem, as distinct from those of married couples. The gap increases with age, so that the rate for cohabitants' children between 11 and 15 approaches that for children of single lone parents (see Table 1, p. 47). Fifty per cent of children with a mental disorder had at one time seen the separation of their parents, compared with 29 per cent of the sample with no disorder. Moreover, children with a mental disorder were twice as likely to live in families rated as unhealthy compared with children with no disorder: 35 per cent, compared to 17 per cent. Among those with a conduct disorder, a background of unsatisfactory, discordant family relations applied to 45 per cent. In line with other research showing higher levels of conflict in families of cohabitants compared to the married, 21 per cent of cohabiting families in this children's mental disorder survey were categorised as showing 'unhealthy' family functioning, compared to 17 per cent of the married and 24 per cent of lone parents.[11]

Differences persist between children of the married and of cohabitants after unions break up. Of American white children between six and 11 years of age living with their mother, twice as many were below the poverty line if she never married, rather than divorced (64 per cent compared with 32 per cent). For blacks, 71 per cent were below the poverty line if the mother never married. This may partly reflect the recruitment of poorer people into cohabitations which produce children, and the decreased likelihood that fathers will pay child support and maintain involvement with children after the relationship breaks up. Attainment also differs. Of children aged six to 11, about 85 per cent of the parents in two-parent or divorced families are high school graduates, compared with 60 per cent of never-married mothers. There appears to be less social capital: even if never-married mothers spend more time with their children, those with divorced mothers are more likely to participate in a range of activities.[12]

All in all, as Sarantakos observes, these findings 'relating to the effectiveness of cohabitation as a dyadic relationship and as a socialising agency show clearly that this lifestyle cannot be compared to marriage. Particularly with regard to its role as a childrearing agency, cohabitation demonstrates serious shortcomings which deserve further consideration'.[13]

Table 1
Prevalence of Mental Disorders by Family Type and Age

Child's age group	Child's family type						
	Married	Cohabiting	All couples	Lone parent single	Lone parent widow divorced separated	All lone parents	All
	Percentage of children with a mental disorder						
5-10-year-olds	6.3	8.8	6.6	15.4	12.9	13.8	8.2
11-15-year-olds	8.6	15.3	9.1	15.5	18.5	17.9	11.2
All children	7.3	11.2	7.7	15.4	15.8	15.7	9.5

Source: *The Mental Health of Children and Adolescents in Great Britain*, Office of National Statistics, 2000.

Chapter 6

No Trial Run For Commitment

Differences in behaviour and outcomes, such as breakdown and satisfaction rates, are to be understood firstly and primarily in relation to essential differences in the nature of marriage and cohabitation. Bluntly: 'The primary difference [from marriage]... is the level of commitment to the partnership'.[1] Whatever the quality of love the couple have for one another, cohabitation is essentially a personal and ultimately provisional agreement between two individuals which does not acknowledge any wider responsibility. With marriage, expressions of long-term or lifelong commitment are made publicly before family, friends and the community at large, while cohabitation is private and thus more easily reversed—the difference between a whole-life with a term insurance policy.[2] While changes to divorce law have made marriage something which may be 'entered or left, as a matter of individual choice', this is not the same as saying that it has become nothing but 'a subjective experience [i]n the private domain'.[3] To those involved, the 'piece of paper' still indicates a publicly expressed commitment and symbolic change of status. If vows of permanence and fidelity are an important part, then:

> ...marriage as an institution is historically based on a fundamental realisation—that all affective ties between men and women, no matter how biologically based they may be, are notoriously fragile and breakable ... In large measure, these promises are designed to bind males to long-term commitment in order to foster social fatherhood.[4]

By closing the gap between natural and social parenthood, marriage has traditionally tied a man's position in the wider society to the proper performance of family duties, by relating him to the children born to a particular woman whom he is obliged to care for. Moreover, marriage is an institution where the pursuit of individual objectives is replaced by joint goals, or, in economic jargon, joint utility-maximisation by husband and wife.[5]

As such, marriage is acknowledged by the public at large. In the Eurobarometer Survey1995 commitment and the rights of children are important elements in the impetus to marry.[6] When asked about their level of agreement to a list of 11 reasons for getting married, the top response related to committing oneself to being faithful to your partner (79 per cent agreeing in the UK); the next to marriage being 'the best way to guarantee the rights of the children' (45 per cent); and the third was 'to prove to the other person that you really love him/her'(39 per cent). The importance accorded to these factors did not vary much by gender, marital status or past history of cohabitation. When Ros Pickford compared married and cohabiting fathers, she found that the most likely reason given for marriage by married fathers was wanting to make or demonstrate a commitment. Almost six out of ten of the married fathers gave this as the reason, while only one in ten unmarried fathers gave it as the reason why they might marry. However, as if distancing themselves somewhat from direct commitment to their partner and the relationship, children were given as the foremost reason for marriage among unmarried fathers.[7] In Susan McRae's study, the most important reason given by cohabiting women who married after becoming mothers was to ensure the security of their children.[8]

Michael Johnson has identified three different experiences of commitment, defined as behaviour that involves supporting and maintaining the continuation of a relationship. First, a personal commitment relates to feelings about *wanting* to continue a relationship, depending greatly on the satisfaction obtained.[9] Second, there is the moral commitment, where people feel that they *ought* to continue, derived from a sense of what is right and wrong. Third, there is structural commitment which relates to feelings that one *has* to continue. This results from the investment of time or effort in the expectation of long-term gains, when these are returned or reciprocated. 'When partners are committed they are able to make assumptions about the future and consequently they tend to view the practice of everyday married life slightly differently'.[10] If marriage as an institution brings with it external constraints to ending the relationship, so barriers to leaving emerged as a significant predictor of relationship breakdown.[11] This adds emphasis to the (unpopular) view that the stability of relationships needs to be looked at with regard to the pressures that prevent people leaving a relationship.[12]

Commitment involves the creation of something extra, a supra-entity beyond the immediate relationship of two individuals, or a partnership which can persist despite the condition of their relationship. People who say that '...a piece of paper at the end of the day and a ceremony and having a lot of people[...] it doesn't change the way you feel about each other',[13] are only seeing one bit of the picture:

> The partnership was the joint project of the partners, the purpose of staying together. It anchored their relationship and in turn their relationship—the emotional attachment between them—sustained their partnership. At times when the relationship was not going very well the partnership was crucial

because it articulated their future commitment—'things aren't great but what would be the point in breaking up because this is really why we are together'. Commitment is expressed as a commitment to the partner and to the enterprise of building a life together.[14]

As such, the 'benefits of a good relationship require time... The sense of being committed and being the focus of another's commitment, buys that time'. Without this constraint, relationships are open to drift, and may falter in the face of difficulties, whatever the investments in children and property: '[h]aving children together makes parents of couples. It does not necessarily create partnerships'.[15] Interestingly, cohabitants rarely refer to themselves in terms of a partnership, tending to interpret commitment only in terms of the ongoing relationship one to another.[16]

While a relationship is private, a partnership is social and recognised by others. Commitments embodied in law may still have greater durability, not least because of the greater barriers to terminating these. Because of this, married individuals may be more likely to solve their problems, or at least arrive at acceptable compromises, than cohabiting individuals whose relationships are less enforced by social and legal constraints. Steven L. Nock used a sample from the US National Survey of Families and Households[17] (as cohabitations do not endure as long as marriages, the analysis was limited to relationships of no more than ten years duration, and, even then, the average length of the marriages picked up in the sample was almost twice that of cohabitations). He found that cohabiting males and females were more apt to report that ending their relationship would have more positive and fewer negative consequences than did either people who married directly or cohabited and then married. Those who married after cohabiting were closer to those who married without cohabiting than those who were currently cohabiting.

Almost by definition, cohabitants are less committed to stable and enduring relationships.[18] Becoming a couple without the constraints and complications of marriage offers more freedom where there is an inability or unwillingness to take on the responsibilities, and potential liabilities, involved with commitment. Cohabitants enjoy freedom from rules regarding entry into and exit from the unit, and a wish to be able to determine one's own family affairs without interference on the part of the authorities is, to an extent, a factor in almost all cohabitation, as this 'may allow individuals or couples who feel unready for the demands of marriage to delay the assumption of marital roles but to acquire the benefits of co-residence'.[19] Professional commitments may be seen as irreconcilable with marriage, parenthood and household schedules, which will restrict individuals in their efforts to involve themselves fully in their career, while cohabitation is felt to be more reconcilable with career because it is precisely perceived as *not a family*. In turn, married people are seen as having to act as a unit, relying on each others resources, while cohabitants are independent, or just 'loving friends'.[20] Cohabitation particularly allows men to avoid parenthood and 'escape from responsibilities by leaving relationships or re-negotiating them when children are born'.[21]

As such, cohabitation offers some of the advantages or functions of marriage in terms of economies of scale, companionship and sexual relations. Sotirios Sarantakos emphasises that, while structural and ideological conditions have created the environment conducive to establishing cohabitation as an alternative to marriage and justifying this, still:

> The reasons for living together unmarried ... can be reduced to one major reason, factor, or cause: namely *convenience*. Legal, economic, social, personal, or sexual convenience are the driving forces which lead to cohabitation. Marriage is avoided because in this lifestyle convenience is coupled with legal responsibility and commitment, which cohabitants want to avoid at all costs.[22]

In his study, 23 per cent of cohabitants stated they were 'very committed' to their relationship, compared to 64 per cent of the married, with 32 per cent of the cohabitants compared with two per cent of the married 'uncommitted'. The majority of cohabitants thought marriage more committing than cohabitation, felt that cohabitants were less committed than marrieds, and that they would have been more committed had they been married.

Temporary or indeterminate partnerships, where permanency is avoided, give individuals freedom from some of the restraints of marriage, they do not afford experience of marriage, however much it 'apes marriage and thus creates the external appearance of a union of lives without creating the internal, moral, legal, or emotional reality of such a union'.[23] The attraction lies in the lack of legal and other ties, and in the ease of negotiating or separating, if the partner does not fulfil one's needs, or other circumstances dictate that the relationship be abandoned. It might be said to involve a different 'bargain' compared to marriage, with cohabitants expecting less mutuality and sharing:[24]

> ... the nature and choice of partner not only indicates the presence of purpose and commitment in the relationship, but it also defines the seriousness of the relationship, sets criteria of selection which correspond to the needs for and expectations associated with permanence, and guarantees some degree of compatibility of the partners.[25]

The refusal to make a commitment to the mutual care and shared resources of a family 'generates the expectation that "family-like" relationships are temporary, and so unworthy of the investment of time and energy', which the parties are less likely to give or require.[26] If nothing else, uncertainty makes investment in the relationship with this partner much riskier even than in contemporary marriage. All this helps explain why cohabitation tends to be a relationship without a future, or one that lasts for a period of time and then ends, either through marriage or dissolution.[27]

Does It All Come Down To Money?

Such conclusions are repudiated by those who deny that marriage *causes* higher stability and commitment, and would rather see marriage as simply symbolising a reflection of economic conditions. According to this view, it 'is important not to confuse the formal institution with its substance for to do so risks creating the illusion that the institution generates the social context with which it is associated'. Thus, it is illusory that marriage supports parenthood, since people marry when their 'socio-economic circumstances are such that their chances of providing the most favourable social capital for their children are at their highest.[28]

It is true that, when the man has a poor economic situation at the time of the formation of a partnership, he is more likely to cohabit. Couples are less likely to commit themselves in the face of uncertain prospects, or when the economic gains from marriage are low or negative. Prudence has dictated that a couple should wait until they are financially secure enough to 'afford' marriage, without which children should not be produced. In the past, this meant attenuated courtships. Now a couple can move in together and even produce children while the nuptials are put off or abrogated in the absence of the financial security felt necessary for marriage.

If marriage were just a certification of a couple's economic achievement or security and had no special relationship to reproduction, it would hardly be so ubiquitous in time and place. However: 'In all known human societies, extant or historical, men and women have entered into formal reproductive alliances between individuals of opposite sex. In other words, they have *married*'. In the co-operative rearing of offspring, 'couples forge a powerful commonality of interest' analogous to that existing between blood relatives. Features characterising marriage in all or virtually all societies relate to:

> ...mutual obligation between wife and husband. There is the right of sexual access (often but not invariably exclusive). There is an expectation that the relationship will persist through pregnancy, lactation and child rearing ... there is some sort of legitimization of the status of the couple's children. These... features of human marriage seem so commonplace as to hardly warrant

enumeration, but it is worth remarking that they represent a typical departure from the mating practices of most other mammals.[29]

The marital relationship may be an economic union, but one that can 'only be understood as ultimately reproductive', and as much can be said of the economic activity or the resources accumulated or allocated by the pair. Moreover, while human societies have differed in their requirements or qualifications for marriage, many of which are economic, marriage does not consist in the paying of a bride price or dowry, or the acquisition of a piece of land or a secure job, and so forth.

Even if economic insecurity or unpredictability has a general association with cohabitation, a distinction can still be made between cohabitants who do and do not have marriage plans or intentions. Thus, US researchers have found cohabitants without marriage plans not to differ financially or be more weighed down by other liabilities than cohabitants with plans to marry, but it is the latter who seem more able to sustain intimate relationships.[30]

If marriages tend to be happier than cohabitations, then much of the difference in quality, as well as quantity, has been attributed to differences in the commitment involved. Commitment is an important predictor of a number of variables that reflect the positive aspects of personal relationships, so that spouses who are more committed tend to be also more accommodating toward one another: to communicate and solve their problems more effectively, and to be more content. Happily married couples report that commitment is one of the most important factors in the success of their marriage.[31] 'Commitment to spouse reflects an attitude toward one's partner that is positive, goal-oriented, and loving, and that promotes his or her well-being ...[where-as] variables associated with lower commitment to one's spouse ...seem to have in common a self-focus that precludes the pursuit of shared marital goals and mutually satisfying interactions.' Moreover, a commitment to marriage reflects 'attitudes regarding moral conduct and personal integrity-factors that may lead spouses to remain committed for commitment's sake. [This] ...appears to be founded more on the spouse's sense of right and wrong and perhaps less on the quality of the marriage'.[32] Both these types of commitment seem to be precluded or reduced by cohabitation.

In turn, while both sets of relatives have acknowledged interests in their offspring's marriages, there is no non-marital equivalent of a son-in-law or mother-in-law. The 'private domain' and the institutional framework of society are hardly separable. However it might be wished otherwise, the marital institution is instrumental in generating 'the social context with which it is associated'. Institutions, whether marriage or private property, embody and sustain systems of meaning,

organise and stabilise various practices and arrangements and provide
people with reference points outside their own consciousness that give
coherence and continuity to their efforts.[33] It is very difficult for people
to cobble together their own lives, making up their own rules as they
go along, and continually figuring out how everything is supposed to
work.[34]

Chapter 7

In Search Of What?

When cohabitation is presented as a trial or a substitute for marriage, it is at the very least unclear whether or not there is to be adherence to a code of marital conduct on the part of those without the 'piece of paper'. A 'trial run' can mean that the partners are still on the look-out for other possibilities or a better match, so that they essentially stay in the marriage market or on the dating game—still available rather than 'spoken for'. Uncertainty about the other party is combined with the prospect that a more suitable partner might become available in the future. In Ros Pickford's sample, 41 per cent of the unmarried fathers had not married their child's mother because their relationship was unsatisfactory, but were not opposed to marriage if the 'right' woman came along.[1] Cohabitation is a lifestyle in itself, rather than a step to marriage or preparation for marriage. Moreover, while there is 'a widely held hypothesis that cohabitation leads to a type of interaction which increases the development of interpersonal skills of the partners, which are important for maintaining heterosexual relationships', how might these develop if:

> ...the relationship lasts only for a short period and is followed by a new relationship of the same type [and] the cohabitors have no opportunity to adjust to the system and learn interpersonal skills or marital roles, which result from maturity and experience.[2]

As James Q. Wilson puts it:

> There is no way to prepare for the commitment other than to make it. The idea that a man and a woman can live together without a commitment in order to see if they would like each other after they have made the commitment is preposterous. Living together may inform you as to whether your partner snores or is an alcoholic... But it is not a way of finding out how married life will be, because married life is shaped by the fact that the couple has made a solemn vow before family and friends that this is for keeps and that any children will be their joint and permanent responsibility. It changes everything.[3]

As absurd, but commonplace, is the situation where one partner will not commit until they are certain that the other is committed. Pathetically, the women in Carol Smart's and Pippa Stevens' study were described as:

> suspending full commitment until they could see that the father of their child(ren) had changed into a more responsible partner/father ... while the

women wanted their men to become more 'marriage-worthy', because they did actually want marriage, it is far less clear what the men were waiting for and far less clear that they wanted marriage at all.[4]

Even if the partners could be said to be 'testing' their compatibility in some way, a partner thought to be suitable for the more flexible purposes of cohabitation would not necessarily be thought suitable for marriage.[5] Sarantakos found that only eight per cent of his sample selected a partner for the purpose of marriage. For 45 per cent, the selection was directed towards finding a partner who would live together with them unmarried, and who should therefore be an adequate cohabitant rather than a potential marriage partner. For some, who were often separated or divorced and with children, and where a partner was badly needed in the one-parent family, trust and reliability were emphasised, as cohabitation was a way of establishing a quasi-marriage which was felt to be either impossible or irrational to formalise. (They may have suffered in a previous marriage and did not want to go through divorce again, or could not afford to lose benefits or a pension.) For others, the ideal partner was a person who would agree to live together without commitment or responsibility, with each partner's personal and social freedom preserved in all circumstances and with complete freedom to leave the relationship at will—which was explicitly declared not to be a marriage.

> Lynn: I knew that I was not going to marry ... For this reason I was trying to meet somebody who would like to share his life with me without complications. I didn't want to get a husband. I wanted a person who could be a good partner, who would love me, respect me, and who would agree to go through good and bad times with me... I didn't want children, and he shouldn't want children either.[6]

Another respondent emphasised how:

> The minimum I expected from him to be was trustful, loving and compatible. I didn't think more about it, if it did turn out to be a wrong decision I could get away at any time.

Sarantakos observes how, taking into account its purpose, the process of cohabital selection was well planned, well thought out, goal-oriented, and well justified. The intention was to establish a relationship that would offer pleasure and immediate gratification, sexual and social convenience, without future orientation. In the 47 per cent of other cases, selection was directed at choosing a friend for the purpose of spending free time together: 'It was rather a way of securing a relatively permanent dating partner, who could obviously be replaced later by another partner.' Many of these unions did not possess the required commitment and will, or the standards of partner selection, to make either cohabitation or marriage work.

Men, in particular, may believe that cohabitation allows them to keep their independence and avoid the economic and other disadvantages of marriage. Significantly, when cohabitants in the US National Survey of Families and Households were asked about how they thought their lives would differ if they married, nearly a third of men (but only a sixth of women) reported that 'their freedom to do what they want' would be reduced.[7]

All this leaves much room for ambiguity and ambivalence, and so scope for disagreement and confusion on the part of one or both parties as to what the relationship is supposed to be and where it is going. Certainly, a substantial minority of cohabiting couples disagree about the future of their relationship. Such a lack of concordance may affect the quality of the relationship as much as its stability. In the US National Survey of Families and Households a fifth of cohabiting persons did not expect to marry anyone, let alone their current partner, and there was disagreement over whether marriage might occur in about one-fifth of the couples in which at least one partner expected this. Hence, 'instability ... is not surprising when we consider that about a third disagree about marriage or do not expect to marry'.[8] This was higher for cohabitants from previous relationships. These were more inclined to report trouble in the relationship and decreased plans to marry where their partner had children by someone else, while cohabitants with their own children were prone to 'wishful thinking', and had a markedly increased expectation of marriage to their partner! A sizeable proportion of women (but not men) fancied that their economic and emotional security would improve if they married, as would their overall happiness.[9] Even in the absence of express desires for marriage, or when ideologically opposed to this, Carol Smart and Pippa Stevens observe that few women enter cohabitation/motherhood without any sense of commitment or hope that commitment might evolve in such a way as to make their relationship more positive and lasting. They hoped, only to be disappointed, that:

> things would 'work out', that stability will grow, or that partners will change their behaviour with the passage of time.[10]

It may not therefore be surprising that, in Sarantakos' sample, only 43 per cent of cohabitants felt 'secure' or 'very secure' in their informal relationship, compared to 91 per cent of marrieds. The rest felt insecure—like Pauline, who have lived with David for four and a half years:

> You don't know how long it will last for, even if you do your best to please him. You can't be sure whether there will be a tomorrow with your partner in the first place... But you have to accept things as they are, I suppose ... it affects you in many ways. You cannot plan for the future, you cannot think of buying a car together or a house, to have a child, or even to love him fully, if you know that tomorrow he may not be there...[11]

Insecurity was reported to cause anxiety, tensions, frictions, and conflicts between the partners. In some cases, these reinforced existing grievances which adversely affected the quality of interpersonal relationships. Men were usually the object of the criticism, and they argued in turn that women's demands were unreasonable and impossible. After all, cohabitation for them was not meant to offer security, but freedom.

> Wendy: I was wrong and I know it. All that stuff about freedom and independence are empty words... it did offer convenience and freedom all right, but only for Jim. De facto relations as an arrangement works for the males and not for us ... After six months I could realise how this relationship was putting me deeper into insecurity and exploitation. I was investing my time and effort looking after him, I was neglecting my career, and had nothing in return, except that I could leave him at any time, which for me was far from a privilege... This is not a reward for our contribution to our families but an easy escape for males... I don't regret having lived in it. I have learned a lot from this experience. Living in this arrangement offers a lot of freedom to one partner to exploit the other.[12]

Or, in the words of another woman:

> It can go on indefinitely. A lot of people will say we'll see how it goes and one year turns into five years and you see people on Ricki Lake with five kids and there's still not commitment.[13]

There may be more conflict and violence in cohabitations because some cohabit rather than marry 'to keep more of their independence, only to find that there are frequent arguments over rights, duties, and obligations'. Admission that 'the marriage license may also be a control license',[14] suggests that successfully controlling another or being controlled may be more problematic in cohabiting than married relationships. When people are more committed to one another, they 'may "give in" to their partner's wishes, believing that they need to make sacrifices or compromises for the sake of keeping the relationship intact'. As seen, cohabitants appear to lack a relative ability to control each other's behaviour, as with alcohol and drug consumption. On the contrary, these may be a means of asserting power. Men concerned with demonstrating their masculinity may try to accomplish this symbolically through drunkenness, dominating women and exerting physical force. Male alcohol consumption as a prime cause of cruelty towards women and children has long historical antecedents, but marriage may constrain conflict from escalating because the costs of potential violence may be greater for married compared to cohabiting couples. Having greater material, social and psychological investment in the relationship, the married see this, and the other partner, as more 'worthwhile' to preserve, and wish to avoid the risks of termination or loss. If, for cohabitants, the relationship ends as a result of aggression, they will not suffer as much as married people, who have greater long-term interests. Moreover, where children are involved, David Blankenhorn agrees with Martin Daly and Margo Wilson in their cross-cultural study of homicide, that the 'institutional inhibitor of male violence [is] paternal investment through an alliance with the mother'. Without this, there is an unstable and highly combustible mixture of 'sexual proprietariness, concern for offspring, resentment, and relative powerlessness, all operating without the benefit of any institutional coherence or structure. It is a seedbed for male violence'.[15]

Chapter 8

Living Down To Expectations

Couples who enter cohabiting unions may have different attitudes towards marriage and divorce compared with those who do not.[1] In particular, there may be a high proportion of individuals with unconventional attitudes or deviant lifestyles, or with less respect for marriage, or who conform or adapt less to marital expectations. Some of the couples in floundering cohabitations might never have lived together at all 'in a more marriage-oriented society, and it may be that current attitudes to marriage give some of these uncertain relationships a better opportunity to establish themselves as a family unit'.[2] With less people marrying direct, this will apply especially to those who cohabit without a prior intention of marrying their current partner, or who did not envisage marrying them at all. Otherwise, as a 'trial' relationship, cohabitation may attract those who are more accepting of the termination of intimate relationships, a tendency which may carry over to greater acceptance of divorce. If attitude translates into action, then people who place less importance on marriage and see divorce as an acceptable alternative, would have greater risks of subsequent divorce if, and when, they do marry.

Responses to the Eurobarometer survey describing what marriage might mean, show how cohabitants are more likely than those who married directly to agree with statements describing the restrictive nature of marriage and less likely to agree with statements about the advantages of marriage (see Table 2, p. 68)

Subtly, the choice between marriage and cohabitation will be affected by attitudes and values towards work, family, leisure, money and sex roles, as well as attitudes concerning marriage itself.[3] While a few cohabitants may oppose marriage on ideological grounds, believing it to be oppressive, there are more general 'liberal values' here, which represent:

> ...more than a political orientation. Rather... these values are indicators of preferences for a kind of union with distinctly different characteristics than marriage. ...cohabitation is attractive as an alternative to marriage not only because it is a tentative, nonlegal form of a coresidential union but, more broadly, because it accommodates a very different style of life.[4]

For young men, the importance of success and steady work have effects on the probability that they will form a union and that the union will be a marriage rather than a cohabitation. For men concerned with money *per se* the effects are in the opposite direction, given that they are likely to see marriage as a financial drain because it gives spouses claims on each other's earnings and assets. Women who value money and career success for themselves are also drawn to cohabitation. Men to whom leisure time for their own pursuits is important may find marriage unappealing, so, if they form a union, this increases the probability that it will be a cohabitation.

William G. Axinn and Arlene Thornton used a 23-year, seven-wave study from Detroit[5] of young people and their mothers to investigate the role of attitudes in the relationship between cohabitation and susceptibility to divorce. They found that, while endorsement of marriage decreased the rate of cohabitation, acceptance of divorce increased it. Those who agreed strongly with divorce (as the best solution when people have marriage problems) and the proposition that people should not stay in marriage for the sake of the children when they do not get along, entered cohabiting unions at a rate 144 per cent higher than those who disagreed strongly. Attitudes did not affect overall union formation, only the choice between marriage and cohabitation, so that those with a high commitment to marriage were more likely to choose this over cohabitation, while those who found divorce more acceptable were more likely to choose cohabitation over marriage.

Similar results were obtained from a 14 year data span of the National Longitudinal Study of the High School Class of 1972, which permitted analysis of first union formation from late adolescence to the early thirties.[6] After all controls for personal characteristics and family background, favourable attitudes towards marriage increased the probability of forming a first union in a given year quite substantially, or more than doubled it. The same importance attached to marriage also significantly lowered the probability that the union would be a cohabitation, or from 22 per cent to seven per cent for men at younger ages and from 22 per cent to four per cent for women between those who thought marriage 'not important' to those who thought it 'very important', with even greater gaps at later ages.

When parents have more favourable attitudes to divorce, or less favourable attitudes to marriage, both may be transmitted to their children and lead to higher rates of both cohabitation and divorce. There appear to be intergenerational effects of maternal commitment to marriage and acceptance of divorce which are not explained by the children's attitudes. In William G. Axinn and Arlene Thornton's study, daughters of mothers who believe that married people are happier cohabit at significantly lower rates than daughters of mothers who believe otherwise.[7] Thus, cohabiting was only 31 per cent as high for daughters of mothers who agree strongly that married people are happier, as for daughters of those who disagree strongly. Daughters of mothers who would be bothered if they did not marry cohabit at significantly lower rates than daughters of mothers who would not be bothered if they did not marry. The effect on sons of mothers' attitudes was much smaller, although those with mothers who agreed that married people are happier also seem to marry at a higher rate than sons of mothers who disagreed.[8]

Similarly, in Paul R. Amato and Alan Booth's analysis of the Study of Marital Instability over the Life Course, parents' 'nontraditional' attitudes and behaviour increased the chances that offspring cohabited either prior to, or instead of, marriage. Moreover, offspring who began cohabiting relationships between 1980 and 1992 were more likely to end these relationships without marrying if parents were reported as 'nontraditional' in 1980. In particular, mothers' full-time employment increased the likelihood of relationship dissolution by 131 per cent for both sons and daughters.[9] (And of their married daughters divorcing by 166 per cent.)

Parents who divorce may also set an example about the desirability or necessity for marriage, so that it becomes downgraded or marginalised for the children. As an aspect of the strong association between family structure and future family formation, children who experience parental divorce are more likely to cohabit, less likely to marry directly and more likely to have children outside of marriage, as well as more likely to divorce in turn. From countries like Sweden where cohabitation is general and normative to Italy where it is still comparatively rare, it is always the case that, if women experienced the separation of their parents, they are more likely to cohabit.[10] 'The consistency of this association between parental separation and cohabitation across nations suggests that this finding might be added to the litany of robust associations with respect to contemporary demographic behaviour'.[11] In turn, in all countries, women who did not experience a parental divorce are more likely than those who did to have their first child within their first marital partnership. Conversely, in all countries, except Sweden, those who experienced parental divorce during childhood were more likely to have a child within a cohabiting union than those women without such an experience.[12] Thus, in the Study of Marital Instability over the Life Course, parental divorce and marital instability or 'divorce-proneness' were both strongly related to their offspring's cohabitation. An increase of one point on the parental divorce-proneness scale was associated with a 178 per cent increase in the odds of cohabitation. Put simply, the children of divorced parents are much more likely to cohabit than to marry.[13] In this study, parental divorce did not appear to increase the risk that offsprings' cohabiting unions would break up—unlike offsprings' marriages, where parental divorce increased their divorce rate by 76 per cent—only their greater tendency to enter a more unstable type of relationship.

Unhappiness, conflict or turmoil at home, following on from parental break-up and leave taking, perhaps with pressure from new partners to move out, may make youngsters quick to move in with someone offering attention and accommodation.[14] Not only, as might be expected, is early residential independence from parents associated with cohabitation, but early initiation of sexual activity. Those whose first coitus occurs in a relationship that neither is nor becomes domestic are more likely to cohabit when they do form residential unions.[15]

> [C]ohabitation may meet the needs of adult children of divorce (and those from intact but unstable families) especially well [because] these children may be emotionally needy or may seek out relationships as a way to escape from an unhappy home environment. On the other hand, young adults from divorced families ... are often wary of making life-long commitments. Cohabitation meets these conflicting needs by providing an emotionally supportive relationship, but one without the legal entanglements and life-long expectations of formal marriage.[16]

The family may be a significant determinant of an individual's choice of whether or not to cohabit, but it is not the only reference group when it comes to the orientation and evaluation of people's thoughts and actions. There are also peers, churches, media and others which may not only promote views which differ from those of individuals' families, they may also be in competition for allegiance. Whether or not their views prevail depends on the comparative influence they wield over the individual, with peer influence increasing in line with falling parental involvement and rising family breakdown. For Australia, Sarantakos found that the most frequently mentioned reference group among marrieds was the family, and among cohabitants the peer group, whether there was just these two alternatives to choose from or a far wider range. Cohabitants choose peers at more than double the rate of the married, and vice versa for the family.[17]

Cohabitation As A Screening Process

Cohabitation may also disproportionately attract people with less of the personal skills, inclinations and attributes required for a stable or successful partnership.[18] It might be risky to grant certain people any formal position, or rights, in one's life, so that the mentally disordered, eccentric, addicted, and so forth, are only accepted as partners with a status like that of a casual flatmate—to help with the rent or house-work and alleviate loneliness. Education, training, employment, or the lack of it, may not only dictate that marriage is best postponed, or avoided, but there may be little or no intention of a long-term relationship of any kind, as when people are students. Cohabitation in such circumstances is geared to having a companion and/or resident sex partner, for the time being, not a spouse.

These, as well as other factors already considered, suggest that the screening mechanisms employed in the search for a suitable match may be less vigorous for cohabitation compared to marriage, with couples quickly sliding into live-in relationships without evaluating whether they are really suited. The speed with which people may move in with each other—perhaps precisely on the understanding that 'if it does not work, little is lost', or that it can or will be left when circumstances change—makes cohabitation worse at guaranteeing compatibility. This may mean that consensual unions are characterised by levels of uncertainty and commitment that make them more like 'going steady' or even 'experimental dating'.[19] One French study found that, when first moving in, the majority of couples had not thought about marriage.[20] In Australia, a fifth of cohabitants had been involved in their relationships three months or less before moving in, another 25 per cent had known each other four to six months, and another 28 per cent seven to 12 months.[21] Another study, in Sweden, found that, over time, there was a quadrupling from six to 25 per cent of women forming first unions with men they had known for less than six months, so that 'the first period within a consensual union has surely to some degree replaced the previous practice of going steady'.[22] As much has been born out by investigation of reasons for cohabitation in Australia, where the respondents often perceived themselves as too young or immature for marriage, unsure about their own or their partner's level of commitment, compatibility or interest, but exploring intimate relationships and wanting to spend time together while making economies.[23] Overall, 'drifting into cohabitation' was the most common way of establishing cohabitation in Sarantakos' sample.[24] Time spent in one household increases, so that the partners find themselves spending most of their time (including nights) together. This makes the keeping of both households irrational and expensive. A merger occurs, whether as part of a gradual evolution, or after discussion of the conditions of the relationship.

As it has become evident that couples move in together simply because they are attracted to each other to some degree, this has led researchers to retreat from notions of cohabitation as any form of 'trial marriage'. Instead, it has been increasingly described as a step or stage in the 'courtship process', or that cohabitation is often more realistically seen as an alternative or substitute for other adult non-family living arrangements, like living alone or with unrelated housemates, rather than marriage.[25] When patterns of 'partner choice' for cohabiting and married couples have been compared to test whether cohabiting unions were 'informal marriages' or 'looser bonds', the latter designation has been found more appropriate.[26] Such considerations and the fact that, on a number of scores, cohabitants are closer in behaviour to single people than the married, has led to conclusions that, despite great 'heterogeneity among American cohabitors, we maintain that, taken as a whole and in this time frame, cohabitation in the American context is primarily an alternative to being single'.[27]

Marriages preceded by cohabitation, rather than entered directly, tend to be less satisfactory as well as more fragile. Social and economic determinants of cohabitation account for some of the lower stability. But if such marriages are also characterised by low levels of commitment to the institution of marriage, and low marital quality, then these are also independently linked to the higher likelihood of divorce.[28] While cohabiting relationships tend to be less satisfactory than marriage, either or both partners may come to believe that getting married may make poor relationships work. As we saw, there is often disagreement or misunderstanding between the couple on the future of the relationship. One party (usually the woman) may manoeuvre the other into marriage, but a signature on the register does not necessarily mean that he has entered into the spirit, as well as the form, of marriage:

> Couples in which one spouse places a high value on autonomy and the other spouse places a low value on autonomy and couples in which one spouse has strong external motives for being married and the other spouse has weak external motives for being married are likely to experience stress as constructed expectations, assumptions, and standards for the marriage become violated. In time, this stress may develop into 'irreconcilable differences'.[29]

This may help explain why long cohabitations (of two years or more) seem to be particularly associated with breakdown of the current marriage. In this as well as other ways, cohabitation may select couples who are less likely to be satisfied when married, rather than filtering out the less compatible.

A Formative Experience In Itself?

The nature of cohabitation, along with the characteristics of the people it is most likely to attract in terms of their attributes and attitudes, may not be all that is needed to explain the poorer marital relationships for previous cohabitants. This may also owe something to the experience of cohabitation itself as well as the types of people who choose to cohabit and the ways in which cohabiting relationships are formed. Cohabitation may teach people something about relationships that changes the way individuals view marriage and divorce, having a 'knock-on' effect which reduces commitment to marriage itself as a lifelong relationship. It may not only attract the divorce-prone, but experience of it could foster divorce-prone attitudes, or values that make divorce more acceptable as a solution to problems, so that cohabitation itself may have a causal influence on susceptibility to divorce. The increase in divorce risk for those who have previously cohabited in another partnership prior to marriage persists when other characteristics, like higher levels of pre-marital childbearing or less traditional attitudes to marriage and divorce, are taken into account.[30] Certainly, one explanation for the higher divorce rate of prior cohabitants is that 'escape' is perceived as the foremost answer to problems. They also retain more permissive sexual attitudes and acceptance of sex with women and men other than their spouses.[31]

A further longitudinal study of attitudes towards family formation at age 18 and age 23, which included a detailed history of living arrangements, found that cohabitation significantly altered attitudes towards family formation in early adulthood, something not found for other non-parental or independent living arrangements, whether living alone, with unrelated house-mates, or in institutional arrangements. As this increased young people's acceptance of divorce, so the more months of exposure to cohabitation that young people experienced, the less enthusiastic they were towards marriage and having children.[32] The differences may be a result of the way in which cohabitation means social interaction with a person who will be, on average, less enthusiastic about family life than others (or is effectively being selected for holding negative attitudes to marriage and family life), as well as a product of simply living with someone in an intimate relationship without being married. A cohabiting person who is highly committed to marriage is, on average, likely to have a cohabiting partner who is less committed, or negative, towards marriage. To the extent that this indicates more negative attitudes towards families in general, or to childrearing, contact with cohabiting partners may have more impact on family formation attitudes than other independent living situations. Young people who have cohabited desire significantly fewer children than young people who have not, while the actual experience of living with a child had no effect on fertility preferences. In turn, the experience of dissolving a cohabitation appears to have the same attitudinal effect as ending a marriage: both lead to more positive attitudes towards divorce.

This relationship is challenged by researchers like David R. Hall who claims that, when attitudes towards relationships are statistically controlled for, pre-marital cohabitation no longer predicts divorce.[33] His findings from the Canadian Fertility Survey of 5,315 women aged 18 to 49 in 1984 are that women who live 'common-law' before their first marriage have a third greater risk of divorce at any time in their marriage than women who do not cohabit before their first marriage. The attitudes which he believes account for the high risk of marital instability concern favourable views on 'pure relationships' (as delineated by Anthony Giddens) where self-satisfaction is paramount and involve, for example, permissive attitudes on reproductive technologies, abortion and the separation of childbearing and childrearing from marriage. Women who strongly approve of 'pure relationships' have about a 75 per cent higher chance of getting divorced than those with only moderate approval. To the extent that these attitudes give form to their marriages, these will be inherently unstable, with a high risk of divorce even where there has not been cohabitation before marriage.

However, attitudes towards intimacy are not only brought to personal relationships, but can be shaped by experience: Hall's study uses a retrospective, and cross-sectional sample, not one traced over time. This cannot distinguish the effects of attitudes and values on cohabitation from the effect of cohabitation on attitudes and values. In contrast, Sarantakos found for Australia that multiple pre-marital experience with cohabitation seemed to be associated with larger proportions of married couples reporting low commitment.[34] In turn, the high rates of termination which accompany cohabitation serve to reinforce the idea that intimate relationships are fragile and temporary. Worryingly, such studies suggest that: 'once this low-commitment, high-autonomy pattern of relating is learned, it becomes hard to unlearn'.[35] In a review of evidence on the causes of marital breakdown for the Lord Chancellor's Department, Lynda Clarke and Ann Berrington cautiously admit that: 'It would seem that any protective effect that cohabitation has in acting as a weeding mechanism is being outweighed by a selection effect, and also possibly by the effect of cohabitation itself on the individual's attitude to marriage'.[36]

Since behaviour alters attitudes, this suggests that new experiences with living arrangements may play a role in reshaping family formation values generally, where residence patterns in early adulthood may have influenced changes in family formation attitudes.[37] It is normal to expect people who are single, married, parents, childless, or divorced to become more positive towards these situations after they have experienced them. Even individuals who do not enjoy or desire an experience or who feel that it is wrong, may develop more favourable attitudes as a way of rationalising their own previous choices or situation as an attempt at dissonance control.

Table 2
Percentage of EU respondents endorsing each of various statements that 'getting married means...', by relationship status in 1993

	Married (%)	Currently Cohabiting - First Union (%)	Currently Cohabiting, and Previously Cohabited (%)	Previously Cohabited, Currently Single (%)
Committing yourself to being faithful to your partner	66.5	62.9	49.6	46.2
Proving to the other person that you really love him/her	46.8	32.5	21.7	24.7
Coping with difficulties more easily	38.2	24.8	15.2	18.4
Making day-to-day living easier	29.6	20.2	12.6	16.0
Committing yourself to a future with some-one who might develop differently from you	18.5	20.2	27.6	28.9
Making a possible break-up more difficult	16.1	22.1	34.9	23.4
Needlessly changing a private relationship into something official	12.3	23.8	30.4	19.9
Giving in to social pressure	5.8	16.2	21.9	13.7
Getting stuck in a routine	6.1	9.6	12.0	11.4

Source: Eurostat, 1995 (Eurobarometer poll, 1993)

Chapter 9

Afraid To Love Without A Net

The evidence so far gives no comfort or support to popular beliefs that cohabitation is a better relationship, or that pre-marital cohabitation leads to a better marriage, or is a way to reduce divorce. It is not suggested that cohabitation *necessarily* leads to a bad marriage, or is *necessarily* a low-quality relationship. However, 'pre-marital cohabitation does not improve the choice of marital partners; does not offer an enriched courtship where partners get to know each other and gain experience of matters related to marriage, does not offer much opportunity to test the compatibility of the partners...'[1] If you live together before marriage, you will not have a stronger marriage than if you don't live together. In fact: 'no positive contribution of cohabitation to marriage has ever been found'.[2] As it is, there are more couples with pre-marital cohabitation than without, 'demonstrating a low marital satisfaction, low marital happiness and interpersonal dependence, domestic violence, marital conflicts and instability'.[3] While cohabitation is never actually helpful, it is at its most innocuous, or has no adverse effects on subsequent marriage, when both partners are definitely planning to marry, so that it effectively coincides with the engagement period.

Failed or broken cohabitations are not a way to learn to have better relationships. Multiple cohabiting, where one or both partners has had prior experience with cohabitation, is a strong predictor of the failure of future relationships and an increased likelihood of divorce. Those who have experienced one partnership breakdown have a higher risk of experiencing the dissolution of a subsequent partnership. Paradoxically, longer cohabitation is not more successful cohabitation, but is associated with unsatisfactory relationships (whether or not in subsequent marriage), as the low commitment ethic takes hold.[4] In the evidence on the causes of marital breakdown for the Lord Chancellor's Department, Lynda Clarke and Ann Berrington warn that, as increases in cohabitation among never-married individuals will result in increasing proportions of individuals beginning marriage after having experienced the breakdown of one or more previous co-residential unions, there is a '...need to examine the increase in cohabitation in terms of consequences for relationship stability and the implications for children'.[5]

In general, cohabiting relationships tend to be less satisfactory than marriage relationships. In allowing more flexibility and freedom, cohabitation positively exposes people to conditions that are likely to generate problems in the relationship. While cohabitation is seen as a way of minimising the risk of family disruption and domestic violence, it paradoxically increases their likelihood.[6] Moreover, the evidence gives no support to dominant political beliefs that cohabitation is equal to marriage as a relationship or childraising unit. Cohabiting parents break up at a much higher rate than married parents, with all the adverse effects of break-up on the children, plus a greater chance of losing the absent parent's support and contact than with a former marriage. Children are also disadvantaged in that cohabiting couples have a lower level of household income, which is probably both a cause and effect of cohabitation. In turn, children living in cohabiting unions are at a higher risk of abuse, including lethal violence, than are children of marital unions. Families underpinned by lifelong commitment provide the most stable and enduring environment in which children can grow, emotionally, physically, mentally and intellectually.

Nevertheless, it might be argued that cohabitation is ethically superior to marriage because it is genuinely free commitment without binding formalities. However:

> If one's wish is to commit oneself, there is no ethical superiority in committing oneself less than one could. Cohabitation is ideal for the partner who is less committed. It is fine as long as relations are good: when there is tension it is the scoundrel's excuse and the dependent's bane.[7]

It has been said that cohabitation is what lovers do when at least one of them does not dare to 'love without a net'.[8] The emphasis on self-investment and protecting oneself against relationship failure militates against mutual dedication and support.[9] A case can be made that cohabitation:

> is far more threatening to marriage as an institution than mere promiscuity could ever be. Merely having sex, even with a man one loves, is not at all like being married. And so pre-marital sex does not blur the line between marriage and unmarriage nearly as much as cohabitation. Cohabitation apes marriage and thus creates the external appearance of a union of lives without creating the internal, moral, legal, or emotional reality of such a union. The result is highly destabilising not just for marriage as an institution, but for the young men and women who mistake a substitute for the real thing .[10]

It can be argued that the poor performance of cohabitation as a socialising agency and dyadic relationship is a significant contributor to the general 'crisis' of adult relationships: feeding into a self-reinforcing inter-generational cycle of relationship failure.

Cohabitation now 'straddles courtship and the early stages of marriage, deferring marriage but also to varying degrees engagement, "going steady" and even, if convenience dominates and commitment is minimal, experimental dating'.[11] While 'it is doubtful that some contemporary dissolutions of consensual unions are any different from time-honoured break-ups of boyfriend/girlfriend relationships', they nonetheless have more of an impact, and a negative one at that, on male/female relationships.[12] Being able or prepared to move in quickly together leads to poorer mate selection and less compatibility. Unlike courtship, where the parties retain some distance and autonomy, there is less room to manoeuvre. Most relationships 'are practice' and, in a culture which allows dating and free social contact between the sexes, 'people have many more relationships than they have marriages. Not (or not only) because they're finding the right person; because they are learning how to do it'.[13] Unlike courtship, cohabitation affords less ease of withdrawal or disengagement if things go wrong. Attachment is a strong and basic drive, and a process as likely to be present in a mismatch as elsewhere.[14] Despite the instability of cohabitation, cohabitants take it for granted that they will stay in the relationship —leading inevitably to confusion, self doubt and 'feelings of disappointment, disenchantment and injustice among many cohabitants when so many of these relationships dissolve'.[15] This destructive process is recognised by Anthony Giddens as a problem with the 'pure relationship'. Thus:

> In heterosexual marriage in earlier periods past sexual encounters were normally 'written out' by both partners as of little significance for the future.

Now:

> A person with whom a partner was in a previous relationship might live on in the minds of one or both; even if prior emotional ties have become quite thoroughly broken, a current relationship is likely to be permeated by their residues. If it be recognised that all adult personal attachments recall aspects of infantile experience, so also do experiences of loss; and in the domain of pure relationships individuals must often now cope with multiple passages of this sort.[16]

In contrast, successful dating or a relatively long engagement may provide experience of equal or more value as a 'trial' for marriage. Traditionally:

> Betrothal was a distinct phase, a liminal situation, between being single and being fully married. Psychologically it enabled each party to move out of the homosocial world, that is, of socialising only with others of the same gender, into the heterosocial world of marriage with the expectations that it carried. Betrothal marked a period of seclusion for the couple so that they could think through and gather resources together. It was also a period of making sure that the match was suitable in all senses.[17]

While cohabitation can be seen in the context of the greater complexity and uncertainty of the modern path into adulthood, its rise has probably had more influence on family formation than changes in other living arrangements. Recent trends in divorce and cohabitation are probably linked in at least two ways.[18] Increasing divorce rates are self-sustaining because they produce an increasing toleration of divorce and a declining commitment to marriage, and thus more divorce. This may be important in the substitution of cohabitation for marriage. In turn, experience with cohabitation, or exposure to cohabiting partners, may have a feedback effect, changing people's attitudes towards marriage and increasing acceptance of divorce—and thereby increasing the likelihood of actual divorce.[19] Perversely, rampant divorce seems to emphasise the importance of trial runs for marriage in order to avoid disruption, or of holding out for the ideal match to come along or avoiding commitment until one is really sure. It may seem to expose marriage as an empty shell, where promises broken are worth less than promises not made at all.

Yet, this is all as much or more likely to feed the cycle of lowered commitment and increased breakdown. Fear of divorce encourages informal relationships as people try to avoid the stresses and financial losses this portends in terms of property and, for men, maintenance or child support—so further weakening marriage as an institution.

This makes cohabitation an important engine behind the decline in marriage as a lasting union, a major stage in the adult life-course, a source of meaning and order in life, and the primary institution governing childbearing and parenthood. Describing a self-reinforcing cycle, Paul R. Amato and Alan Booth speak of how the results from their Study of Marital Instability over the Life Cycle suggest that the increase in cohabitation is at least:

> ...partly propelled by the dramatic increase in divorce, as well as marital instability in the parental generation. Given the continuing high divorce rate... we can expect to see frequent and early cohabitation among young adults in the forseeable future. But because these relationships tend to be unstable, a high rate of cohabitation is accompanied by a high rate of relationship turnover.[20]

This decline in marriage might be more positive if it meant that fewer couples would have to endure bad marriages and painful divorces. However, the divorce rate is at an historically high level and has stayed there. As such, the collapse of marriage means growing family instability and declining investment in children, as it also leads 'not only to serial partnerships but also towards more *separate* lives for men and women', manifest not only in lone parenthood, but the fast growth in men living alone.[21] This betokens the 'growing incoherence of paternity... As marriage weakens, more and more men become isolated and estranged from their children and from the mothers of their children'.[22]

The unintended consequences of what are often attempts to circumvent the hazards of family breakdown, given modern pessimism about the chances of marital success, have more to do with the actual decline in marriage than any fanciful ideological rejection on the part of the public at large, involving their invention of new, preferred 'family forms'. And, while the increasing trend towards 'consensual partnering' might be taken by dominant opinion as evidence of emancipation from oppressive or rigid concepts of marriage, it can equally or better be seen to manifest 'declining commitment within unions, of men and women to each other and to their relationship as an enduring unit, in exchange for more freedom, primarily for men'.[23]

The extent and nature of public confusion over cohabitation is telling, with the same factors simultaneously seen as both advantageous and disadvantageous. About a half of never-married, childless cohabitants under 35 see cohabitation favourably as a 'trial marriage', and its benefits are generally perceived in terms of the lack of legal ties and financial obligations. Wanting to have the cake they were eating, nearly a half of cohabitants also mentioned financial insecurity as a drawback and the lack of legal status, commitment and social recognition were also seen as disadvantages. Women were more likely than men to see the down side.[24]

Chapter 10

Why Discriminate Against Cohabitation?

The regular calls to give cohabitation the same status as marriage are driven by a tangle of beliefs, with contradictory premises and goals. The assumption is often made that marriage and cohabitation are really indistinguishable, or that it is only outmoded legal and other distinctions which are maintaining any differences. The Lord Chancellor's Department is anxious that family law 'adequately reflects modern social attitudes and conditions' and that this '...falls within the wider context of the Government's commitment, set out in its pre-election manifesto, to uphold family life as the most secure means of bringing up children'.[1]

There is the well-intentioned notion that equal recognition and treatment will lead to the greater stabilisation and success of cohabitation. Since relationships are in increasingly short supply, why not support these in whatever form they occur, or recognise 'commitment' where ever we find it—like the Advisory Board on Family Law, which believes that when the father puts his name on the birth register this constitutes 'an appropriate degree of commitment to the child', which should be acknowledged.[2]

Making marriage and cohabitation synonymous for all practical purposes is also meant to fully affirm the changing, serial relationships that are in line with the development and demands of plastic sexuality and expressive individualism. The obverse is that attempts to strengthen or preserve marriage are futile, as the tide of modernity is running against it. Thus, while in most cases cohabitations have no future, cohabitation must necessarily become the basis of future society, with 'dangers for social stability' threatened 'if we are afraid to look critically at whether policy supports all family units in the best possible way, now that marriage has lost much of its power for many people'.[3] In particular, giving 'a legal role as parents' to cohabiting men (or initially to those who declare themselves on the birth certificate), or all genitors, and therefore departing from the age-old grounding of fatherhood in marriage, will somehow lead to better parenting by reinforcing both commitment and underpinning a future of transient adult relationships. Withholding affirmation from cohabitants, or unwed fathers, 'does not seem to offer support to a vulnerable group of relationships and arguably works to undermine the objective of promoting a sense of involvement and responsibility among these fathers which cannot benefit their children'.[4] Surely such affirmation would blend social justice and compassion with the goal of personal freedom by helping to create a level playing field for all relationships, in order that choice might be unconstrained and fully realisable. This means being completely non-prescriptive as well as non-discriminatory, so that, even if a society without norms is likely to 'face a variety of problems', it would 'be better placed to allow individual men and women opportunities to define for themselves appropriate ways of living'.[5]

Not least, law and public policy, which previously supported marriage, must intervene to prevent support for marriage, or eradicate bias or 'discrimination on the basis of marital status'. Apparently, it 'is not possible to 'promote marriage as the best family form, without undermining non-married families'.[6] As marriage is demoted culturally from: 'foundation stone to just another lifestyle, about which we all are supposed to remain neutral in comparison to other lifestyles',[7] any special provisions or protection are seen as unjustified since marriage is no more than a matter of the personal choice and satisfaction of the two people involved, and because these are somehow a denial of the equal validity of other lifestyle choices, as well as of 'equity' or 'social justice'. Thus:

> ... as the civil rights group Liberty said in relation to the green paper: 'The reality is that some relationships and family structures have the Government seal of approval and some don't. This is insulting to single parents and their children, as well as to lesbian and gay parents—who are just as likely to create happy, stable families as anyone else'.[8]

Even where it is found that '...the framework of marriage is associated with the establishment of a joint parental relationship which frequently continues beyond the termination of the marriage', and while 'marriage may therefore be a desirable context for parenthood in its reflection of and association with resources and stability and might properly be encouraged', it is still insisted that parental obligations should not be grounded in the institution of marriage, but related to 'the fact of parenthood', since parenthood outside marriage would otherwise be disadvantaged.[9]

As it is, the state has been 'slowly admitting cohabitation as an informal marriage status',[10] and gradually recognising this, in virtually every nook and cranny of law which has an impact on domestic relationships. If marriage has moved towards receiving less social and legal recognition, cohabitation has moved in the opposite direction, particularly as marriage-like benefits are beginning to go to cohabiting couples. A series of legal decisions has given the formerly cohabiting partner claims on jointly occupied property, provided she has made some input into its acquisition or maintenance. There are rights in the occupation of the home similar to the married in the case of domestic violence under the Family Law Act 1996, and succession rights on death for the surviving cohabitant under the Law Reform (Succession) Act 1995. In the attempt to provide for gay and lesbian couples who cannot marry, some businesses or institutions are providing 'domestic partnership' benefits ranging from health insurance and pensions to free travel and the right to inherit accommodation. In the process, these benefits are usually offered to unmarried heterosexuals as well in order to avoid accusations of sex discrimination. This is seen as testimony to the way in which family law:

> ... has abandoned much of its punitive and negative character and presents an appearance of gender neutrality and non-interference. It is less concerned with legal status than with economic reality. Marriage is being displaced by 'family' and the wife is being displaced by the mother.[11]

In turn, 'family' is being defined as any, or even no, domestic relationship (as when someone who lives alone is seen to comprise a 'family', or be part of a 'family' in that they must be related to somebody). Thus, two men have been deemed a 'family' for the purposes of Rent Act protection. Official equality has probably gone farthest in France where, in 1999, live-in partners, heterosexual or homosexual, could enjoy virtually the same tax, social security, property and inheritance rights as the conventionally married. All they have to do is to register their union at a local court. To end this, the couple notify the authorities and the union is dissolved in three months. If the split is not mutual, the departing partner just serves a letter on his or her mate. This arrangement was originally supposed to fulfil the Government's pledge to give legal recognition to homosexual partnerships where, after a parliamentary battle, the provisions were extended to opposite-sex couples. This demonstrates how difficult it is to bring in public recognition for homosexual unions without creating a low-commitment institution for heterosexuals at the same time, or vice versa. It is not surprising that much of the pressure to recognise cohabitation, or legitimise unions outside of marriage, comes from gay activists.[12]

If marriage is assumed to serve no useful purpose, then it makes sense to ground public policy on the 'fact of parenthood', as this flows from the idea of supporting all children, regardless of family structure, as of simply supporting 'families' without seeming discriminatory or making 'value judgements'. Taking this 'fact of parenthood', as the recognised basis of family life will allow for expression of that infinite diversity of 'new family forms'.

However, the enforcement of some form of proposed 'parenthood contracts' opens up nightmare prospects. Fathers will presumably have access to various households to do their bits of serial 'parenting', when the evidence is hardly positive when it comes to the potential of parenting from different addresses and relationships. Men who have refused to marry the mother may then be obstructive in exercising their parental 'rights' from afar, without being fathers in actuality. In particular, there is the loss of social capital for the child, which is:

> ... an asset that is created and maintained by relationships of commitment and trust. It functions as a conduit of information as well as a source of emotional and economic support, and can be just as important as financial capital in promoting children's future success. The decision of parents to live apart— whether as a result of divorce, or an initial decision not to marry—damages, and sometimes destroys, the social capital that might have been available to the child had the parents lived together.[13]

When a father lives in a separate household, he is usually less committed to his child and less trusting of the child's mother. He becomes less altruistic towards, or less closely identified with, the children, and thus less willing to share his income and time with them, or to invest in their welfare. He may develop new attachments which supersede previous ties, creating loyalty conflicts, where not everybody can come first. 'Can a culture that refuses to insist that men and women accept the sacrifices of marriage credibly insist these same people make large sacrifices for the sake of unmarriage?'.[14] Family disruption may reduce a child's access to social capital outside the family by weakening connections to other adults and institutions in the community that would have been available to the child had the relationship with the father remained intact. When two parents share the same household, they can not only better monitor the children and maintain parental control, but they also create a system of checks and balances where they monitor one another and make sure the other parent is behaving in appropriate ways. Currently, there is much emphasis on the adult/child bond, with the belief that this can be maintained and improved independently, despite the lack of the adult/adult bond. However, the first is dependent upon the second, so that when the parent/parent bond is good, so too is the child/parent bond; there being 'a power in that bond between adults which can cradle the relationship to children'.[15] When the adult/adult bond is unreliable, unsatisfactory, or broken, this has adverse effects on the parent/child bond. Given that 17 of the 40 respondents in Carol Smart's and Pippa Stevens' study only started to cohabit when a birth was imminent, and so therefore had no 'joint project' or clearly established commitment to the other partner prior to the birth, or separation, 'parents can sometimes be virtual strangers, or even antipathetical to each other very quickly after they become parents. It is hard to see how parents can jointly parent after separation if they have not had the opportunity to do so during their cohabitation'.[16] Studies on the relationship between the amount of access to the non-residential parent and child adjustment are ambiguous. Some show benefits, others none and a few find negative relationships.[17] Unfortunately, evidence from large, nationally representative surveys indicate that frequent father contact has *no* detectable benefits for children when they live apart.[18]

More widely, the implications for people's well-being of entering and leaving multiple relationships are depressing. Emphasising how ending relationships is stressful for all parties involved and how singlehood is associated with low levels of psychological health, the authors of *A Generation at Risk* consider that 'a pattern in which people shift frequently from one relatively short-term intimate relationship to the next is unlikely to be one that maximises the happiness of the next generation'.[19]

If the idea is that public affirmation might keep people together, it raises the question: affirmation of what? After all, cohabitants have deliberately (even if temporarily) rejected the ties of marriage and chosen cohabitation *because* it is easier to walk in and out of and *because* it appears to give the individual freedom from the responsibilities and restrictions of marriage.[20]

Giving cohabitation the same status as marriage will subject cohabitants to a regime they are trying to avoid. Is it possible to seek freedom from responsibility and commitment in cohabitation, and at the same time seek assistance in the courts to claim rights from a relationship which was not meant to be legally binding in the first place? More broadly, if institutional freedom is considered paramount, state intervention undesirable, and self-regulation desirable in relationships, there are no grounds for regulating cohabitation. It is arguable that, even if cohabitation becomes legally more restrictive, this will hardly make it equal or better than marriage 'Cohabitation will still carry its cultural and social heritage. Which will make it a second rate marriage'.[21]

The regulation of cohabitation will open the way to regulating and recognising other relationships as sources of rights. If this means homosexual unions, then why not non-sexual partnerships, whether between people of the same or opposite sex, such as two friends or brothers and sisters? Cohabitation is difficult to define, and investing rights in cohabitants would be a considerable source of contention, as well as creating increased expenditure for business and communities. Cohabitants are presently as free as anyone else to make wills and bequests, for example, and can jointly own or rent their home. In turn, the Children Act 1989, introduced a new procedure for an unmarried father to acquire parental responsibility, defined as 'all the rights, duties, powers and responsibilities and authority which by law a parent of a child has in relation to the child and his property', by making a Parental Responsibility Agreement with the mother, which must be properly witnessed and registered with the court. Alternatively, fathers may apply for Parental Responsibility Orders themselves. There has been a low take-up rate, as people may be ignorant of the law. If, as claimed, three-quarters of fathers do not know that unmarried fathers do not have parental responsibility for their children, then this is an indication of the need for more public information. It is often said that 'hard cases make bad law'. If fathers who find that they have not acquired legal status simply by being a 'natural' father 'think the law should be changed to give fathers in their situation the same status as a married father', should this be sufficient to bring the law into line with these erroneous assumptions?[22]

> Totally outrageous ...me not being married makes me an unworthy parent. I can't look after my own child? ...Well I think, it devalues fatherhood, you know, it, it's taking away some of my role of being her father. Just because the fact that I haven't, you know, I haven't signed a bit of paper.[23]

It might be asked why it is so important to this man not to have signed the 'piece of paper', if that is all you need to do to get parental rights?

There is an assumption that any situation people find themselves in, or anything they endorse, must be affirmed, in a world where there is to be no good or bad, or true or false, and thus no objective reality or coherence. Thus, if unmarried fathers do 'not think that marriage was a relevant criterion for fatherhood', the world must be changed to accommodate their opinions.[24] Sometimes, indeed, a lot of the time, people are wrong, factually, morally, or both. The man who says 'I know Kim wants to get married but I'm fairly happy as I am and I like to say I think Tommy is more of a bond than a bit of paper' is simply wrong, as is the man who claims that: 'As far as bringing up a child is concerned, it [marriage] just is nothing. Nothing whatsoever. Nothing. It doesn't matter one little bit'.[25]

Parental rights for unmarried fathers are not about promoting the welfare of children; the emphasis is on the rights of the adults. The claim that, if people 'think that cohabitation is just a modern, private form of marriage then ...all differences between marriage and cohabitation should be abolished', is just wrong. Marriage cannot be 'private' without abolishing itself.[26]

Since cohabitation affects the married and the institution of marriage, its further institutionalisation needs to be questioned. The regulation of *de facto* relationships in specific areas involves acknowledgement of the problems of cohabitants and legal adjustments to solve disputes between those who have lived together unmarried. Some problems are not specific to cohabitants, be they homosexual or heterosexual. The Law Commission recommends that homosexuals should be able to claim damages if financially dependent upon a partner who dies in an accident caused by someone else's negligence, but this could apply to anyone financially dependent upon another, whatever the nature of their relationship. Moreover, people should be welcome to make 'living together contracts'—in contrast to participating in a legal status created by Act of Parliament—to reduce the uncertainty in the legal system so that, for example, property entanglements are avoided should the relationship break down.[27]

As the alternatives to marriage are strengthened, so the institution of marriage is progressively weakened. This undermines the only institution ever shown to be capable of raising children successfully.[28] This is something expressly intended by many of those calling for the 'level playing field' for all relationships, either by co-opting cohabitation to marital status, or by moves to 'abolish marriage as a legal category, and with it any privilege based on sexual affiliation. With the latter, there would be no special legal rules governing the relationships between husband and wife or defining the consequences of the status of marriage as now exist in family law'. The 'interactions of female and male sexual affiliates would be governed by the same rules that regulate other interactions in our society—specifically those of contract and property, as well as tort and criminal law ... Women and men would operate outside of the confines of marriage... Without the fetters of legalities they did not voluntarily choose [sic].'[29] For its part, the Law Society wants cohabitation contracts to be enforceable, providing that they deal with financial matters and meet certain criteria (like full financial disclosure and after each party has been independently advised), and are revoked or reviewed by events like the birth of a child(ren), or disability. It also wants a legislative framework for those who choose not to make a contract. While maintaining that the latter would focus upon the economic consequences of the relationship rather than looking at what happened before or happens after it, as with divorce, the Society believes that the court's powers to make orders should be modelled on those under the Matrimonial Causes Act 1973 (as amended) so that, for instance, the court would have power to order a lump sum order, property adjustment order, or transfer of property order, and that rights of occupation should be protected (as when cohabitants do not own a share in the home), as for marrieds under the Family Law Act 1996. Similarly, maintenance for cohabitants is meant to shadow the system as applied to the married; pension sharing should apply equally, as should provisions for life insurance; and heterosexual and homosexual cohabitants who have lived together in the same household for two years should have the same claims on the estate of the other, should one die without a will, as spouses under the Inheritance (Provision for Family etc) Act 1975.[30]

At the very least, if the rights of marriage are given to those who do not accept the responsibilities and '...cohabitation gets the same material benefits as marriage, marriage becomes stripped of all incentives...'[31] As it is more simple and less complicated just to live together, the expansion of domestic-partner benefits to cohabitants effectively endorses fragile family forms which pose risks to women and children. What seems to have been quite forgotten is that family concessions and prerogatives, whether travel passes for railway employees' families or pensions for widows, arose from recognition of the costs of childrearing, and the responsibilities that married people had to care for each other and their children and in acknowledgement of the contribution to society made by those who take on these tasks and obligations. None of this applies in the case of friends, companions or paramours. This is not to diminish other relationships, they just do not serve the purposes of marriage, which has already been established as an institution to regulate family relationships.

If the bonds and constraints that sustain and uphold marriage are eliminated, so is marriage as a public institution, no matter what other formalities and rituals might be retained.[32] Marriage offers an alternative way of life to cohabitation. Both are voluntary, and each has its attractions for different people under different circumstances. But if the distinction between them is eliminated, the possibilities or options of life are reduced. Marriage may involve constraints, but it tends to be overlooked that constraints are part of the creation of a 'secure and predictable environment in which real and durable *choices* may take place. When we lose the constraints we lose choice; we lose a species of liberty and the guarantees that underwrite the unique and productive environment that marriage can create'.[33] As the privileges of marriage 'are gradually dissipated in the name of diversity of choice, and only its responsibilities remain, individuals become more reluctant to marry. When its responsibilities also begin to dissolve, then marriage itself begins to disappear'.[34] The recognition and support of unmarried cohabitation, like 'gay marriage', as equal 'lifestyle choices', destroys the rights of the majority of the population to have meaningful marriage. Like a corporation, or private property, marriage has to be publicly supported by law and culture in order to exist. Law and social policy embody, impose and reinforce moral values; these are not self-sustaining and disintegrate without support.

There is the continuing belief that the further deconstruction of marriage will increase its attraction. Finding that one in three cohabiting mothers cited a fear or dislike of divorce which seemingly deterred them from marrying, Susan McRae surmised that, were the divorce process '...less confrontational, or divorce perhaps easier to obtain, then it seems likely that more long-term cohabiting mothers would marry'—when the likelihood is that even less would do so, since even easier divorce would mean more divorces, and thus more fear of divorce.[35] Cohabitation is increasing at a time when legal divorce is more easily obtained than at any time in our history. It is 'no accident that cohabitation emerged as a widespread phenomenon at exactly the same time marriage was being demoted from a permanent commitment, severable only for cause, to a temporary, fully revokable arrangement, terminable at will of either spouse'.[36] While people may feel the law is an irrelevance to the running of their everyday lives, they are often unaware of the extent to which the law shapes the contours of their lives,[37] not least through the incentives structure which it imposes, and the moral assumptions it embodies. The incentives which induce people to marry can change so that they no longer want to stay, or get, married. Since the norms enshrined in law have made marriages provisional and contingent, people behave defensively and are dissuaded from investing in a common enterprise, in each other, and in children. Making marriage less binding than a job contract, no-fault and unilateral divorce encourages opportunism, has lowered the costs to departing spouses and removed protection from spouses who do not want their marriages to dissolve. Not only need the instigators of divorce incur little or no loss, they may benefit. The growth of cohabitation is evidence of the way in which:

> ...people today must plan to be whole and self-sufficient and cannot risk interdependence. Imagination compels everyone to look forward to the day of separation in order to see how he will do ...there is no common good for those who are to separate.[38]

Chapter 11

Back To The Future ... Not

It is argued that cohabitation hardly constitutes a threat to marriage, since it will be the revival of *social marriage*, reflecting ... the modern-day diminishment of social norms which sanctioned only particular ways of living and condemned all others'. However, even were '... marriage in England and Wales [before the Marriage Act 1753] ...largely a private matter between two individuals and their kin', this is not to be equated with informal cohabitation, which was regularly punished by ecclesiastical authorities in many parts of Europe. It is easy to confuse betrothals or conditional, intermediate statuses (which could be terminated by the consent of the parties) with informal marriages, or to believe that the only recognised marriage was in church following the publication of banns. The church may not have always 'insisted upon the posting of banns nor the presence of a priest for the contracting of a valid marriage', but a valid, publicly recognised marriage there was—and one very difficult to rescind, if at all—once the exchange of promises followed by sexual intercourse changed betrothal into marriage.[1] Even jumping over that broomstick was 'carried out in front of witnesses, without the intervention of the church': it was clearly public and the couples were recognised as having commitments to each other, communally policed. Susan McRae herself observes that 'it appears to have been unusual for tally marriages to fail', where 'couples who lived in open cohabitation were careful to behave in ways that were loving, circumspect and conventional', and even that 'their success in doing so and in gaining the approval of family and community provides the explanation for why so little is known about tally couples'.[2] (Perhaps 'tally' couples were also not so common as some now like to think). The reason is that: 'Throughout history, there has never been a time when living together unmarried was generally approved of by the community, as an acceptable way of life'.[3] Some communities practised 'what we might call processional marriage; in other words where the formation of marriage was regarded as a *process* rather than a clearly defined rite of passage'. This might begin with the exchange of promises before witnesses, and was irreversibly confirmed by a pregnancy.[4] Stephen Parker, a primary source on this subject, asserts how a 'recurrent problem in most communities was to ensure a male provider for women and children' and that 'in many cases consent to intercourse and consent to marriage were not separated analytically and were perhaps deliberately blurred in some communities'. This was:

> ...so as to avoid illegitimacy and any consequent charge upon the rates. The man was a husband and obliged to maintain his wife and children. It was not only the community which gained control in this way. The knowledge that a marriage would be locally implied from the fact of pregnancy gave power to women who were concerned that the man might desert them. The approach to sex was therefore far from casual: it was located in a general belief in the ability of public opinion to command obedience to community values.[5]

Flexible and perhaps retroactive forms of marriage 'performed an important function in the community by enabling social *mores* and pressure to create a marriage (and thus support obligations) without the need to force the couple into a church. In was strengthened by the clergy's willingness ... to notarise the marriage retrospectively'.[6] At the same time, couples might evade parental control through an informal marriage since, if this took place before a witness, they could not be unmarried, whether or not this was followed by a formal marriage. In some areas, a couple might terminate the marriage by consent if there was no pregnancy, which occasioned rather than constituted marriage, so that informal marriage more closely resembled betrothal. In the meantime, there were strict duties of fidelity. The Isle of Portland was one such 'clannish place where marriage never took place until the woman was pregnant. Local enforcement was so strong (reluctant males would be stoned out of the island) that there was virtually no illegitimacy there'.[7]

None of this deflects from, but rather all reflects, the 'genius of marriage', as 'through it, the society normally holds the biological parents responsible for each other and their offspring. By identifying children with their parents, and by penalising people who do not have stable relationships, the social system powerfully motivates individuals to settle into sexual union and take care of ensuing offspring.'[8] The Marriage Act 1753, made any marriage in any place apart from a church or chapel, and without banns or licence, null and void, as the previous law which enabled marriages to be made from the simple exchange of promises without official preliminaries was seen as 'facilitating seduction or rashness to the disruption of "great and opulent families"'.[9] Otherwise, the act was opposed because it might discourage marriage amongst the poor, not least by making this more expensive. However, these fears did not arise out of 'concern for the emotional development of the poor', or their right to free sex lives, or to construct 'new family forms'. They arose from concern that the supply of labour would fall with the birthrate, and that the removal of backing from customs that made marriage binding upon conception might be dangerous for women and the rate-payers. 'A young woman is but too apt by nature to trust to the honour of the man she loves, and to admit him to her bed upon a solemn promise to marry her. Surely the moral obligation is as binding as if they have been actually married: but you are by this Bill to declare it null and void'.[10] The rise in the rate of registered illegitimate births between 1750 and 1850 may be due to the continuation of earlier, informal marriage practices whose children could no longer be so easily registered as legitimate. With the Marriage Act 1836, civil marriage 'served essentially the same constituency as informal marriage' did.[11]

Claims about marriage being a recent invention have to be related to the fact that the proportion of out-of-wedlock births to total births was only just over five per cent at the beginning of the nineteenth century. The modern system for the civil registration of births, marriages and deaths was introduced in 1837, and the 'illegitimacy ratio' stood at 6.6 per cent in 1842 when it was first calculated under this system—a high peak. It then fell steadily to stand at four per cent at the beginning of the twentieth century (when it was slightly under three per cent in East London, a very poor working-class area). Apart from the surges associated with war (or six per cent in World War I and nine per cent in 1945), the extra-marital birth ratio remained at four to five per cent of all births until the end of the 1950s. Increasing slowly over the 1960s, it nevertheless hovered at around eight per cent until 1976, when it really began to take off. This does not point to a vast array of 'irregular' or informal unions in previous centuries.

Many of the high numbers of unwed births in recent decades have not occurred in unions analogous to ancient and customary 'informal' marriages, but in circumstances these were expressly meant to obviate: where the man is tardy when it comes to accepting responsibility for the mother and child and there is the prospect of them being thrown onto public funds. But comprehensive support is now available for dependent children, whose low-income mothers are able to marry the state instead. The increasing tendency for cohabitation to end in dissolution, not marriage, together with high divorce and out-of-wedlock childbearing, means that more and more young people are growing up with no personal life experience of successful marriage and no confidence that they could be in an enduring marital relationship. Even before entry to fragile cohabitations, they face prolonged exposure to 'the singles mating culture ... oriented to men's appetites and interests', or sex and low-commitment relationships, making it even more difficult to find suitable marriage mates.[12] At the same time, the vast majority say that they aspire to happy and long-lasting marriages and expect to marry somebody. They also view marriage as a serious form of commitment, as well as an overwhelmingly preferred lifestyle. If one takes into account the large proportion of cohabitations that either change to marriage or dissolve, then the acceptance of cohabitation as an alternative to marriage is limited.

Yet, marriage has lost the support of government, and is neglected and discredited in the media. Young adults, who desperately want to avoid marital failure, find little advice, support and guidance on marriage from peers, parents or schools. Support for marriage is said to be 'intrusive', and politicians must keep out of private lives, not 'pressurise' people or 'force' them to get married. Even mentioning marriage will 'turn off half the classroom that comes from unmarried homes, you have excluded them...',[13] as if any situation people find themselves in, no matter how they arrived there, must be the best one for them in their best and only world, and as if it would shatter their identity and self-esteem to suggest any other options. On this argument, there should be no gardening advice, cook books, self-help programmes, medical advice or even advertisements. The scholarly discourse on the family over recent decades has been strongly anti-marriage, something reflected in the textbooks used in colleges and schools. At best, marriage is treated as a joke in sociology departments[14] and has generally come to be seen as problematic, being usually portrayed as a repressive device to enslave women and curtail people's 'choices'.

Chapter 12

The Meaning Of Marriage

People generally need more information on what makes a relationship happy and lasting, and what to expect from the unit they establish.[1] At present, there is 'widespread ignorance of what marriage means. People increasingly assume it's merely a public declaration of a private commitment between two people [in love], not a social institution whose successes or failures have far-reaching effects on the whole of society'. There is little appreciation of, for example, the effects of marriage on health and wealth, both for individuals and society.

> People tend to be puzzled or put off by the idea that marriage has purposes or benefits that extend beyond fulfilling individual needs for intimacy and satisfaction. In this respect, marriage is increasingly indistinguishable from other 'intimate relationships' which have no social purpose and are also evaluated on the basis of sexual and emotional satisfaction.[2]

The scant consideration given to marriage as an institution, or a public, law-governed system for organising basic human relationships, is reflected in the way that the 1998 Lord Chancellor's Paper is clearly at a loss to understand why male parental status should ever have been dependent upon marriage, and concludes that this must have reflected some kind of arbitrary prejudice. It observes that under the Children Act 1989 an unmarried father must apply to the courts if he is to 'be accepted as "meritorious" parent before being able to acquire parental responsibility for his children' while 'there is no such requirement for mothers, or for married fathers, who in practice may or may not be "responsible" parents'.[3] What is completely missed is that biological and social fatherhood do not coincide for men as they do for women in the absence of marriage, which obliges a man to care for a particular woman and any children that are born to her. As such, paternal responsibility involves incorporating the altruistic constraints embodied in parental care into a cultural role. While some married men may neglect their paternal obligations, this hardly means that men make as dependable fathers outside of marriage or that a child sired outside marriage has the same chance of care, on average, from its natural father as one born inside.

As such, an institution is defined as existing:

> ...at a certain time and place when the actions specified by it are regularly carried out in accordance with a public understanding that the system of rules

defining the institution is to be followed ...The publicity of the rules of an
institution insures that those engaged in it know what... to expect of one another
and what kinds of actions are permissible. There is a common basis for
determining mutual expectations.[4]

As the public system of rules governs entry and exit and defines
people's positions in respect of their rights and duties, powers and
immunities, so traditionally the law has guided, confirmed and
formalised, the rules, the sanctions, the roles and the public under-
standings that have gathered around a practice of a contractually
distinctive kind—the marriage relationship. By marrying, people freely
chose to enter a legally defined institution, in which the law and not
the parties establish the rules of entry and membership. Among the
'mutual expectations' that have defined the contract and the institution, and which impose limitations on conduct, is the presumption by
the parties, and their mutually declared intention, that the relationship will be permanent. It is this which, as we have seen, crucially
distinguishes marriage from cohabitation, which actively seeks to
avoid the public promise of permanent bonding that is characteristic
of marriage. The public affirmation of marriage means that a community, not just those directly involved, is endorsing and approving the
vows for themselves as well as for the couple. People continue to seek
marriage and not cohabitation, because of 'the human urge to immerse
oneself in an open-ended and continuing relationship of mutual care
and intimate involvement...' and in response to:

> ...the presumption of a permanent and onerous commitment, ...the act of
> marriage is seen as offering guarantees of continuity and mutual good faith
> matching the importance of the 'investments' put at stake in a marriage.
> Somewhat like the legal forms available to commercial transactions under well-
> formed law, it is believed to reduce the risks of losing the benefits expected to
> flow from substantial investments. The benefits foreseen in marriage and the
> presumption of its permanence include continuity of exclusive sexual enjoyment,
> constant companionship, mutual care, a jointly supported household, the
> advantages of some division of labour, children, cooperative and stable rearing
> of children, and joint endeavours to advance their interests. None of this is
> possible without emotional commitments and joint investments of time, effort
> and money.[5]

Facilitating such 'joint investments' or reinvigorating marriage
probably stands a better chance of reversing deterioration in child
well-being, adult relationships, social welfare and cohesion than
endorsing transient associations, or trying to enforce parental care in
the absence of supporting institutions. 'The laissez-faire acceptance of
the decline of marriage is premature and unwarranted. No consistent,
widespread effort has been made to reverse this trend. Until such an
effort has been made it is irresponsible to say that nothing can be

done.'[6] Matters of marriage and divorce are no more outside the incentives structure than other individual decisions, and are as likely to change with the benefits and costs of various courses and the barriers to their realisation. Married people fare better economically, given that it is easier to achieve more together than alone, but marriage appears more and more as an economic liability or luxury due to the bias in the tax/benefit system and high rate of divorce. The tax burden has been shifted onto families as the measures which once supported couples rearing children have been progressively removed. Married people are now taxed as if they had the discretionary income of childless singles, and lent upon to generate resources for all other needs, as tax relief is targeted at taxpayers in general and at low-income families, disproportionately single mothers. Families have responded by putting more people into the labour market and working longer hours, cutting back on the number of children, and divorcing more often. Others respond by not marrying at all and, if they do, by not having children. Because of the deteriorating tax position of families, people are getting less from marriage than they want, while a benefit system geared to lone parenthood endorses and encourages family fragmentation and the casualisation of relationships.[7] To give people more choice, the state should enable marriage economically—by allowing, for example, income-splitting for tax purposes, or allowance transferral, so that the expectations and promises inherent in the marriage contract can be fulfilled. Although the law presently treats marriage as something revocable at will by either party, people should be allowed to make a lifelong, permanent commitment. This would entail an end to 'no-fault', non-consensual or unilateral divorce, or anyway, settlements which penalise, rather than favour, the spouse who leaves or behaves badly, putting some power back into the hands of the spouse who maintains the marriage.

Revitalising marriage requires the elimination of the anti-marriage bias currently prevalent in school curricula, and treating marriage as a desirable social good rather than one of many equally valid and viable lifestyles. In 1999, the proposed new curriculum for 'personal, social and health education' made no mention of marriage or two-parent families (although 75 per cent of people, according to one poll, supported the promotion of marriage in schools).[8] Instead, pupils were to be taught about 'the range of lifestyles and relationships in society' and be able to form 'effective and fulfilling relationships which... reflect the diversity of and differences between people' or alternatively 'manage a wider range of relationships as they mature, including sexual relationships'. They were also to learn about 'good parenting, its value to family life and the impact of separation, divorce and

bereavement on families and the need for adaptability'. After objec-
tions, the Education Minister promised to include mention of marriage
in advice to teachers, although this is non-statutory.[9] In the US a
marriage education movement is emerging among marriage therapists,
family life educators, schoolteachers, and some clergy. Married couples
are somewhat less likely to divorce now than several years ago (the
increase in the median age at first marriage has probably had a
positive effect).[10] The rate of unwed births has declined for three years
in a row, although the ratio of unwed and marital births remains the
same and the percentage of children in lone-parent families has
become stable.

Education for successful marriage looks at its social and economic, as
well as emotional and psychological, aspects and sees it as a basic
social institution with many dimensions, rather than mainly from a
sexual or therapeutic or personal standpoint. Education about
marriage means elucidating the nature of commitment, for example,
in terms of permanence and loyalty, rather than current sexual
exclusiveness, or pairing off.[11] As people both value marriage, yet are
well aware of its fragility, it is especially important for them not to be
misled or misinformed, but to know what contributes to success and
what weakens it. People need to be helped to avoid painful and
damaging losses and achieve long-lasting and satisfying relationships.[12] Sadly, at present, while so many people expect their future
marriages to last a lifetime and to fulfil their deepest emotional and
spiritual needs, they are involved in a mating culture that may make
it more difficult to achieve this lofty goal.[13]

Through these and other measures, cohabitation may be contained
in ways that minimise its damage to marriage. The role of the state
ought not be to recognise or institutionalise informal unions, but to
outline the nature and consequences of cohabitation, while accepting
this as a living arrangement in itself, and guaranteeing its freedom
and independence.[14]

Notes

Introduction

1   *1. Court Procedures for the Determination of Paternity 2. The
     Law on Parental Responsibility for Unmarried Fathers*, Lord
     Chancellor's Department, March 1998, p. 15.

2   *1. Court Procedures for the Determination of Paternity 2. The
     Law on Parental Responsibility for Unmarried Fathers*, p. 15.

3   'Cohabitation Proposals for Reform of the Law', Family Law
     Committee of the Law Society, 1999, p. 2.

4   The Advisory Board on Family Law, *Second Annual Report*,
     Lord Chancellor's Office, 1998/99, p. 12.

5   Report, *Daily Mail*, 16 June 1999.

6   Willis, R.J. and Michael, R.T., 'Innovation in family formation:
     evidence on cohabitation in the United States', in Ermisch, J.
     and Ogawa, N. (eds.), *The Family, the Market, and the State in
     Ageing Societies,* Oxford: Clarendon Press, 1994, p. 10.

7   Kiernan, K.E. and Estaugh, V., *Cohabitation: Extra Marital
     Childbearing and Social Policy*, London: Family Policy Studies
     Centre, 1993.

8   McRae, S., *Cohabiting Mothers: Changing Marriage and
     Motherhood?*, London: Policy Studies Institute, 1993, p. 9.

9   McRae, S., 'Cohabitation; a trial run for marriage?', *Sexual and
     Marital Therapy*, Vol. 12, No. 3, 1997, pp. 259-73.

10   Report, *Daily Mail,* 16 June 1999.

11   McRae, 'Cohabitation; a trial run for marriage?', pp. 260-61.

12   Lerner, G., *The Creation of Patriarchy*, New York: Oxford
     University Press, p. 239.

13   Fineman, M.A., *The Neutered Mother and the Sexual Family*,
     London: Routledge, p. 23.

14   Giddens, A., *The Transformation of Intimacy*, Stanford: Stanford
     University Press, 1992. See also Hall, D. R., 'Marriage as a pure
     relationship: exploring the link between pre-marital
     cohabitation and divorce in Canada', *Journal of Comparative
     Family Studies*, Vol. XXVII, No. 1, Spring 1996.

15   Giddens, *The Transformation of Intimacy*, 1992, p. 63.

16   Giddens, *The Transformation of Intimacy*, 1992, p. 195.

17   Giddens, *The Transformation of Intimacy*, 1992.

18   Giddens, *The Transformation of Intimacy*, 1992, p.135

19   Giddens, A., *The Third Way: The Renewal of Social Democracy*,
     Cambridge: Polity Press, 1998, p. 97.

20   See Morgan, P., 'Fidelity', in Anderson, D. (ed.), *The Loss of Virtue*, London: The Social Affairs Unit, 1992; and Fortes, M., *Rules and the Emergence of Human Society*, Occasional Paper, No. 39, Royal Anthropological Institute of Gt Britain, 1983.

21   Giddens, *The Third Way: The Renewal of Social Democracy*, 1998, p. 97.

22   Giddens, *The Third Way: The Renewal of Social Democracy*, 1998, p. 95.

23   Dewar, J., *Law and the Family*, London: Butterworths, 1992, quoted McClean, M. and Eekelaar, J., *The Parental Obligation*, Oxford: Hart Publishing, 1997, p. 10.

Chapter 1: Who Wants To Be A Cohabitee?

1   Sarantakos, S., 'Trial cohabitation on trial', *Australian Social Work*, September 1994, Vol. 47, No. 3 p. 13.

2   Popenoe, D. and Whitehead, B.D., *Should We Live Together? What Young Adults Need To Know about Cohabitation before Marriage*, The National Marriage Project, Rutgers, The State University of New Jersey, Brunswick: New Jersey, 1999, p. 4.

3   Sarantakos, 'Trial cohabitation on trial', 1994, p. 13.

4   Whitehead, B.D. and Popenoe, D., 'Sex without strings, relationships without rings', *The State of Our Unions, The Social Health of Marriage in America*, The National Marriage Project, Rutgers, The State University of New Jersey, 2000, p. 12. [http://marriage.rutgers.edu]

5   Bumpass, L.L., 'What's happening to the family? Interactions between demographic and institutional change', *Demography*, Vol. 27, No. 4, 1990, p. 486.

6   See returns from *Monitoring the Future* conducted annually by the Institute for Social Research at the University of Michigan. In *The State of Our Unions, The Social Health of Marriage in America*, The National Marriage Project, Rutgers, The State University of New Jersey, 1999.

7   Scott, J., Braun, M. and Alwin, D., 'The family way', in Jowell, R., Brook, L. and Dowds, L. (eds.), *International Social Attitudes; the 10th BSA Report*, Hants: Dartmouth Publishing Co., 1993.

8   'How Brown got it wrong over tax and the family', *Mail on Sunday*, 14 March 1999.

9   Smart, C. and Stevens, P., *Cohabitation Breakdown Family*, London: Policy Studies Centre, 2000, pp. 25, 29, 30.

10   'The Millennial Family', National Family and Parenting Institute Survey, conducted by Mori, October 1999.

11   Manning, D., 'The changing meaning of cohabitation and
        marriage', *European Sociological Review*, Vol. 12, No. 1, p. 63.

12   Kiernan, K., 'Family change: issues and implications', in David,
        M. (ed.), *The Fragmenting Family: Does it Matter?*, London: IEA
        Health and Welfare Unit, 1998, p. 53; and Kiernan, K. and
        Estaugh, V., *Cohabitation, Extra-marital Childbearing and
        Social Policy*, Occasional paper No. 17, London: Family Policy
        Studies Centre, 1993.

13   Kiernan, K., 'Cohabitation in Western Europe', *Population
        Trends*, Vol. 96, Office for National Statistics,1999.

14   Carmichael, G.A., 'Consensual partnering in the more developed
        countries', *Journal of the Australian Population Association*,
        Vol.12, No.1, 1995, pp. 51-86.

15   Bumpass, L.L., Sweet, J.A. and Cherlin, A., 'The role of
        cohabitation in declining rates of marriage', *Journal of Marriage
        and the Family*, Vol. 53, 1991, pp. 913-27.

16   Blom, S., 'Marriage and cohabitation in a changing society:
        experience of Norwegian men and women born in 1945 and
        1960', *European Journal of Population*, Vol. 9, 1994, pp. 143-73;
        and Khoo, S-E., *Living Together: Young Couples in de facto
        Relationships*, Collins Dove for the Australian Institute of
        Family Studies, 1986.

17   Sarantakos, S., *Living Together in Australia*, Melbourne:
        Longman Cheshire, 1984.

18   Haskey, J., 'Trends in marriage and cohabitation: the decline in
        marriage and the changing pattern of living in partnerships',
        Population Trends, Vol. 80, 1995, pp. 421-29.

19   Ermisch, J. and Francesconi, M., *Cohabitation in Great Britain:
        Not for Long, but Here to Stay*, Colchester: Institute for Social
        and Economic Research, University of Essex, 1998.

20   *Living in Britain: 1998 General Household Survey,* Office for
        National Statistics, London: The Stationery Office, 1999.

21   *Living in Britain: Results of the 1995 General Household Survey*,
        Office for National Statistics, London: HMSO, 1997.

22   *Living in Britain: 1998 General Household Survey,* Office for
        National Statistics.

23   Haskey, 'Trends in marriage and cohabitation: the decline in
        marriage and the changing pattern of living in partnerships',
        1995, pp. 421-29.

24   Haskey, 'Trends in marriage and cohabitation: the decline in
        marriage and the changing pattern of living in partnerships',
        1995.

25   In Australia, the the proportion of *de facto* couples with
      dependent children varied from ten per cent in the Northern
      Territory to two per cent in Victoria in 1992.

26   Kiernan, K.E. and Estaugh, V., *Cohabitation: Extra Marital
      Childbearing and Social Policy*, Occasional Paper 17, London:
      Family Policy Studies Centre, 1993.

27   Marital status projections for England and Wales, Government
      Actuary's Office, 7 January 1999.

28   Carmichael, 'Consensual partnering in the more developed
      countries', 1995.

29   Popenoe and Whitehead, *Should We Live Together?*, 1999, p. 10.

30   Sarantakos, *Living Together in Australia*, 1984.

31   *The Merits of Marriage*, Christian Action, Research and
      Education, 1998 p. 8.

32   Carmichael, 'Consensual partnering in the more developed
      countries', 1995, p. 62.

33   Sarantakos, *Living Together in Australia,* 1984, p. 93.

34   Carmichael, 'Consensual partnering in the more developed
      countries', 1995, p. 77.

35   Keenan, S., 'And you said you were broke', *The Times Weekend*,
      11 March 2000; and Whitehead, B.D. and Popenoe, D., 'Sex
      without strings, relationships without rings', *The State of Our
      Unions, The Social Health of Marriage in America*, The National
      Marriage Project, Rutgers, The State University of New Jersey,
      2000, p. 12. [http://marriage.rutgers.edu]

36   'Children's needs, coping strategies and understanding of
      woman abuse', *Children 5-16: Research Briefing No. 12*,
      Economic and Social Research Council, Department of Applied
      Social Sciences, University of Stirling, Stirling, April 2000.

Chapter 2: A Fragile And Transitory State

1   Ermisch, J. and Francesconi, M., *Cohabitation in Great Britain:
      Not for Long, but Here to Stay*, Institute for Social and Economic
      Research, University of Essex, 1998.

2   Berrington, A. and Diamond, L. 'First partnerships formation
      among the 1958 British cohort: A discrete time competing risk
      analysis', Paper presented at the European Population
      Conference, Milan, September 1995.

3   Ermisch, J., *Pre-marital Cohabitation, Childbearing and the
      Creation of One-Parent Families*, ESRC Research Centre on
      Micro-Social Change, Paper Number 95-17, 1995, from British
      Household Panel Study.

4   Ermisch and Francesconi, *Cohabitation in Great Britain: Not for Long, but Here to Stay*, 1998.

5   Kiernan, K. and Estaugh, V., *Cohabitation; Extra-marital Childbearing and Social Policy*, Occasional paper 17, London: Family Policy Studies Centre, 1993.

6   Bumpass, L.L. and Sweet, J.A., 'National estimates of cohabitation', *Demography* 26: 615-25, 1989; and Willis, R.J. and Michael, R.T., 'Innovation in family formation: Evidence on cohabitation in the United States', in Ermisch, J. and Ogawa, N. (eds.), *The Family, the Market, and the State in Ageing Societies*, Oxford: Oxford University Press, 1994.

7   Bumpass and Sweet, 'National estimates of cohabitation', 1989; and Willis and Michael, 'Innovation in family formation: Evidence on cohabitation in the United States', 1994.

8   Bumpass, L.L, Sweet, J.A. and Cherlin, A., 'The role of cohabitation in declining rates of marriage', *Journal of Marriage and the Family*, Vol. 53, 1991, pp. 913-27.

9   *Australian Family Formation Study*, Australian Institute of Family Studies, Melbourne, 1991.

10   Kiernan, K., 'Cohabitation in Western Europe', *Population Trends*, Vol. 96, Office for National Statistics, 1999.

11   Sarantakos, S., 'Trial cohabitation on trial', *Australian Social Work*, Vol. 47, No. 3, 1994.

12   Kiernan, 'Cohabitation in Western Europe', 1999.

13   Kiernan, K. and Mueller, G., *The Divorced and Who Divorces?*, CASE paper CASE/7, Centre for Analysis of Social Exclusion, May 1998, p. 16.

14   Ermisch, *Pre-marital Cohabitation, Childbearing and the Creation of One-Parent Families*, 1995; Wertheimer, A. and McRae, S., *Family and Household Change in Britain: A Summary of Findings from Projects in the ESRC Population and Household Change Programme*, Centre for Family and Housework Research, Oxford Brookes University, 1999.

15   Carmichael, G.A., 'Consensual partnering in the more developed countries', *Journal of the Australian Population Association*, Vol.12, No.1, 1995, pp. 51-86.

16   *Marital Status and Living Arrangements*, March 1997, US Census Bureau, 1998.

17   Kiernan, K., *European Perspectives on Non-marital Childbearing*, Department of Social Policy and Centre for Analysis of Social Exclusion, London School of Economics paper prepared for Conference on Non-marital Childbearing, Madison, Wisconsin, 29-30 April 1999.

18   Ermisch, *Pre-marital Cohabitation, Childbearing and the Creation of One Parent Families*, 1995.

19   Haskey, J., 'Having a birth outside marriage: the proportions of lone mothers and cohabiting mothers who subsequently marry', *Population Trends*, Vol. 97, Office for National Statistics, London, 1999.

20   Smart, C. and Stevens, P., *Cohabitation Breakdown*, London: Family Policy Studies Centre, 2000.

21   Smart and Stevens, *Cohabitation Breakdown*, 2000, pp. 23, 30.

22   Ermisch and Francesconi, *Cohabitation in Great Britain: Not for Long, but Here to Stay*, 1998.

23   Ermisch and Francesconi, *Cohabitation in Great Britain: Not for Long, but Here to Stay*, 1998, p. 18.

24   Ermisch, *Pre-marital Cohabitation, Childbearing and the Creation of One-Parent Families*, 1995.

25   Dench, G., *The Place of Men in Changing Family Cultures*, London: Institute of Community Studies, 1996, p. 60.

26   Pickford, R., *Fathers, Marriage, and the Law*, London: Family Policy Studies Centre, 1999.

27   Kiernan and Mueller, *The Divorced and Who Divorces?*, 1998.

28   McRae, S., *Cohabiting Mothers*, London: Policy Studies Institute, 1993, p. 105.

29   Maclean, M. and Eekelaar, J., *The Parental Obligation*, Oxford: Hart Publishing, 1997.

30   Kiernan and Estaugh, *Cohabitation: Extra-marital Childbearing and Social Policy*, 1993.

31   Quoted in *To Have and To Hold:, A Report of the Inquiry into Aspects of Family Services*, House of Representatives Standing Committee on Legal and Constitutional Affairs, Canberra, June 1998.

32   Manning, W.D. and Lichter, D.T., 'Parental cohabitation and children's economic well-being', *Journal of Marriage and the Family*, Vol. 58, 1996, pp. 998-1010.

33   Ahlburg, D.A. and De Vita, C.J., 'New realities of the American family', *Population Bulletin* 47, No. 2, 1992, p. 15.

34   Mare, R.D. and Winship, C., 'Socioeconomic change and the decline of marriage for blacks and whites', in Jencks, C. and Peterson, P.E. (eds.), *The Urban Underclass*, Washington DC: The Brookings Institute, 1991.

35   Korenman, S. and Neumark, D., 'Does marriage really make men more productive', *The Journal of Human Resources*, XXVI-2, pp. 282-307, 1990.

36   Lingxin, H., 'Family structure, private transfers, and the economic well-being of families with children', *Social Forces*, Vol. 75, September 1996, pp. 269-92.

37   Amato, P.R. and Booth, A., *A Generation at Risk*, Cambridge Mass: Harvard University Press, 1997.

38   Ermisch and Francesconi, *Cohabitation in Great Britain: Not for Long, but Here to Stay*, 1998.

39   Santow, G. and Bracher, M., 'Change and continuity in the formation of first marital unions in Australia', *Population Studies*, Vol. 48, No. 3, 1994, pp. 475-96.

40   Smart and Stevens, *Cohabitation Breakdown*, 2000 .

41   Pickford, *Fathers, Marriage, and the Law*, 1999.

42   Dench, *The Place of Men in Changing Family Cultures*, 1996, p. 60.

43   Khoo, S-E., 'Living together as married; a profile of *de facto* couples in Australia', *Journal of Marriage and the Family*, Vol. 49, 1987, pp. 185-91.

44   Pickford, *Fathers, Marriage, and the Law*, 1999.

45   Doyle, C., 'Keeping tabs on the pill', *The Daily Telegraph*, 21 October 1999.

46   Reported in *Reader's Digest*, June 1999.

47   Kiernan, *Cohabitation in Western Europe*, 1999.

48   Buck, N. and Ermisch, J., 'Cohabitation in Britain', *Changing Britain*, Issue 3, ESRC, October 1995; McKay, S., 'New data on life events: the family and working lives survey', *Changing Britain*, Issue 7, ESRC, October 1997; and Fergusson, D., 'Family formation, dissolution and reformation', in *Proceedings of the SSRFC Symposium: New Zealand Families in the Eighties and Nineties*, NZ: Canterbury University, No. 20, November 1987, pp. 15-30. In this longitudinal study of children born in Christchurch in 1977, 43.9 per cent of those in 'de facto' unions experienced family breakdown in the first five years, compared with 10.9 per cent where the parents were legally married. Boheim, R. and Ermisch, J., 'Breaking up - financial surprises and partnership dissolution', Paper presented at the Royal Economic Society Conference 1999, Nottingham.

49   Boheim and Ermisch,'Breaking up - financial surprises and partnership dissolution', 1999.

50 Lindgren, 1997, Research Centre on Population, Helsinki reported by Taskinen, S., 'Family policies in Finland in 1996', in Ditch, J., Barnes, H. and Bradshaw, J., *Developments in National Family Policies in 1996,* University of York: European Observatory on National Family Policies, published by the European Commission, 1998.

51 Quoted in *To Have and To Hold:, A Report of the Inquiry into Aspects of Family Services,* 1998.

52 Kiernan, K.E., *Transition to Parenthood: Young Mothers, Young Fathers: Associated Factors and Later Life Experiences,* Discussion paper Welfare State Programme/113, London: Suntory and Toyota International Centres for Economics and Related Disciplines, London School of Economics, 1995.

53 Maclean and Eekelaar, *The Parental Obligation,* 1997.

54 Quoted in *To Have and To Hold:, A Report of the Inquiry into Aspects of Family Services,* 1998.

55 Kiernan, *Cohabitation in Western Europe,*1999.

56 In their sample of 694 'women/year' observations, John Ermisch and Marco Francesconi, observed how women in employment, like those with a partner in a job, were less likely to dissolve their union. Similarly, if a couple received income support, the main means-tested benefit, they had a higher rate of dissolution. Ermisch and Francesconi, *Cohabitation in Great Britain: Not for Long, but Here to Stay,* 1998.

57 Ermisch and Francesconi, *Cohabitation in Great Britain: Not for Long, but Here to Stay,* 1998, p.143.

Chapter 3: Cohabitation And Lone-parent Families

1 Ermisch, J., *Pre-marital Cohabitation, Childbearing and the Creation of One-Parent Families,* ESRC Research Centre on Micro-Social Change, Paper Number 95-17, 1995, from British Household Panel Study. The fastest growing group of lone parents is never-married mothers—the proportion doubling since the mid-1980s from 24 per cent to 42 per cent in 1997 (as the divorced declined from 44 to 33 per cent. [*Family Change: Guide to the Issues,* Family Briefing Paper 12, London: Family Policy Studies Centre, 2000.]

2 Personal communication from An-Magritt Jenson, Norway.

3 Hoem, B., 'One child is not enough: what has happened to Swedish women with one child born in 1936-60?', *Stockholm Research Reports in Demography,* No. 25, University of Stockholm.

4 Kiernan, K., 'Cohabitation in Western Europe', *Population Trends,* Vol. 96, Office for National Statistics,1999.

5   Willis, R.J. and Michael, R.T., 'Innovation in family formation:
        evidence on cohabitation in the United States', in Ermisch, J.
        and Ogawa, N. (eds.), *The Family, the Market, and the State in
        Ageing Societies*, Oxford: Clarendon Press, 1994, p. 24.

6   Kiernan, K., 'Family Change: Issues and Implications', in David,
        M. (ed.), *The Fragmenting Family: Does it Matter?*, London: IEA
        Health and Welfare Unit, 1998, p. 53.

7   Kiernan, K.E., *Transition to Parenthood: Young Mothers, Young
        Fathers: Associated Factors and Later Life Experiences*,
        Discussion paper Welfare State Programme/113, London:
        Suntory and Toyota International Centres for Economics and
        Related Disciplines, London School of Economics, 1995.

8   Carmichael, G.A., 'Consensual partnering in the more developed
        countries', *Journal of the Australian Population Association*,
        Vol. 12, No. 1, 1995, pp. 51-86.

9   Bumpass, L.L., Sweet, J.A. and Cherlin, A., 'The role of
        cohabitation in declining rates of marriage', *Journal of Marriage
        and the Family*, Vol. 53, 1991, pp. 913-27.

10   Wertheimer, A. and McRae, S., *Family and Household Change
        in Britain: A Summary of Findings from Projects in the ESRC
        Population and Household Change Programme*, Centre for
        Family and Housework Research, Oxford Brookes University,
        1999.

11   Ermisch, J. and Francesconi, M., *Cohabitation in Great Britain:
        Not for Long, but Here to Stay*, Institute for Social and Economic
        Research, University of Essex, 1998.

12   *Living in Britain: 1998 General Household Survey*, Office for
        National Statistics, 1999.

13   Ermisch and Francesconi, *Cohabitation in Great Britain: Not for
        Long, but Here to Stay*, 1998, p. 8.

14   *Living in Britain: 1998 General Household Survey*, Office for
        National Statistics, 1999.

15   Kiernan, *Cohabitation in Western Europe*, 1999.

16   Booth, A. and Johnson, D., 'Pre-marital cohabitation and
        marital success', *Journal of Family Issues*, Vol. 9, 1998, pp. 255-
        72.

17   Axinn, W.G. and Thornton, A., 'The relationship between
        cohabitation and divorce: selecting or causal influence',
        Demography, Vol. 29, No. 3, August 1992, p. 358.

18   Haskey, J., 'Pre-marital cohabitation and the probability of
        subsequent divorce', Office of Population Censuses and Surveys,
        Population Trends, Vol. 68, Summer 1992.

19   *Australian Family Formation Study*, Australian Institute of Family Studies, Melbourne, 1991.

20   Hall, D.R. and Zhao, J., 'Cohabitation and divorce in Canada', *Journal of Marriage and the Family*, Vol. 57, 1995, pp. 421-27.

21   Thomson, E. and Colella, U., 'Cohabitation and marital stability: quality or commitment?', *Journal of Marriage and the Family*, Vol. 54, 1992, pp. 259-67.

22   Kiernan, K. and Mueller, G., *The Divorced and Who Divorces?*, CASE paper CASE/7, Centre for Analysis of Social Exclusion, May 1998.

23   Kiernan, *Cohabitation in Western Europe*, 1999.

24   Haskey, J., 'Cohabitational and marital histories of adults in Great Britain', *Population Trends 96*, London: The Stationery Office, Summer 1999.

25   Teachman, J.D. and Polonko, K.A., 'Cohabitation and marital stability in the United States', *Social Forces*, Vol. 69, 1990, pp. 207-20.

26   DeMaris, A. and Vaninadha Rao, K., 'Pre-marital cohabitation and subsequent marital stability in the United States: A Reassessment', *Journal of Marriage and the Family*, Vol. 54, 1992, p. 189.

27   Kiernan, K., *European Perspectives on Non-marital Childbearing*, Department of Social Policy and Centre for Analysis of Social Exclusion, London School of Economics paper prepared for Conference on Non-marital Childbearing. Madison, Wisconsin, 29-30 April 1999.

28   Clarke, L. and Berrington, A., 'Socio-demographic predictors of divorce', in *High Divorce Rates: The State of the Evidence on Reasons and Remedies*, Simons, J. (ed.), Research series No.2/99, Vol. 1, 1999, Lord Chancellor's Department.

29   Ford, R., Marsh, A. and Finlayson, L., *What Happens to Lone Parents: A Cohort Study 1991-1995*, Department of Social Services Research Report, No.77, 1998.

30   Fergusson, D., 'Family formation, dissolution and reformation', in *Proceedings of the SSRFC Symposium: New Zealand Families in the Eighties and Nineties*, NZ: Canterbury University, No. 20, November 1987, pp. 15-50.

31   Kiernan, *Cohabitation in Western Europe*, 1999, p. 40.

32   McClean, M. and Eekelaar, J., *The Parental Obligation*, Oxford: Hart Publishing, 1997.

33   Seltzer, J.A., 'Relationships between fathers and children who live apart: the father's role after separation', *Journal of Marriage and the Family*, Vol. 53, 1991, pp. 79-101. See also

Beller, A.H. and Graham, J.W., 'Child support awards: differentials and trends by race and marital status', *Demography*, Vol. 23, 1986, pp. 231-45.

34   Personal communication from An-Magritt Jenson, Norway.

Chapter 4: Troubled Relationships

1   Brown, S.L. and Booth, A., 'Cohabitation versus marriage: a comparison of relationship quality', *Journal of Marriage and the Family*, Vol. 58, No. 3, 1996, pp. 668-78.

2   Thomson, E. and Colella, U., 'Cohabitation and marital stability: quality or commitment?', *Journal of Marriage and the Family*, Vol. 54, 1992, pp. 259-67.

3   Sarantakos, S., 'Trial cohabitation on trial', *Australian Social Work*, Vol. 47, No. 3, 1994.

4   Bumpass, L.L., Sweet, J.A. and Cherlin, A., 'The role of cohabitation in declining rates of marriage', *Journal of Marriage and the Family*, Vol. 53, 1991, pp. 913-27.

5   Sarantakos, S., *Living Together in Australia*, Melbourne: Longman Cheshire, 1984.

6   Amato, P.R. and Booth, A., *A Generation at Risk*, Cambridge Mass: Harvard University Press, 1997.

7   McRae, S., *Cohabiting Mothers: Changing Marriage and Motherhood?*, London: Policy Studies Institute, 1993, p. 9.

8   Ferri, E. and Smith, K., *Parenting in the 1990s*, York: Joseph Rowntree Foundation, 1996.

9   Nock, S.L., 'A comparison of marriages and cohabiting relationships', *Journal of Family Issues*, Vol. 16, 1995, pp. 53-76; see also Brown, S.L. and Booth, A., 'Cohabitation versus marriage: a comparison of relationship quality', *Journal of Marriage and the Family*, Vol. 58, No. 3, 1996, pp. 668-78.

10   Brown and Booth, 'Cohabitation versus marriage: a comparison of relationship quality', 1996.

11   Sarantakos, 'Trial cohabitation on trial', 1994.

12   Sarantakos, 'Trial cohabitation on trial', 1994.

13   Sarantakos, 'Trial cohabitation on trial', 1994.

14   Brown and Booth, 'Cohabitation versus marriage: a comparison of relationship quality', 1996.

15   Smart, C. and Stevens, P., *Cohabitation Breakdown*, London: Family Policy Studies Centre, 2000.

16   US Bureau of Justice Statistics, *Highlights from 20 Years of Surveying Crime Victims: The National Crime Victimisation Survey, 1973-92*, Washington DC: US Department of Justice, 1993.

17   Bachman, R., 'Violence against women', Washington DC: Bureau of Justice Statistics, 1994, p. 6.

18   Marks, N.F. and Lambert, J.D., *Journal of Family Issues*, 1998.

19   Centers for Disease Control and Prevention, *Morbidity and Mortality Weekly Report 43,* No. 8, Washington DC: US Government Printing Office, 4 March 1994.

20   Atkin, B., 'The Domestic Violence Act', *The New Zealand Law Journal*, January 1998, pp. 24-31.

21   Roberts, A.R., 'Psychosocial characteristics of batterers: a study of 234 men charged with domestic violence offences', *Journal of Family Violence*, Vol. 2, No. 1, 1987, pp. 85-95.

22   *The 1998 British Crime Survey,* Home Office Statistical Bulletin, Issue 21/98, Government Statistical Service, 1998.

23   Martin, D., *Battered Wives,* San Francisco: Glide, 1976, p. 37.

24   Gelles, R.J. and Straus, M.A., *Intimate Violence*, New York: Simon and Schuster, 1989.

25   Stets, J.E. and Straus, M.A., 'The marriage license as a hitting license: a comparison of assaults in dating, cohabiting, and married couples', in Straus, M.A. and Gelles, R.J., *Physical Violence in American Families*, New Jersey: Transaction, 1995 p. 227; see Yllo, K. and Straus, M.A., 'Interpersonal violence among married and cohabiting couples', *Family Relations*, Vol. 30, 1981, pp. 339-47.

26   Sarantakos, 'Trial Cohabitation on Trial, 1994.

27   Dench, G., *The Place of Men in Changing Family Cultures*, London: Institute of Community Studies, 1996, p. 36.

28   Stets, J.E., 'Cohabiting and marital agression: the role of social isolation', *Journal of Marriage and the Family*, Vol. 53, 1991, pp. 669-80.

29   Huffman, T., *et al.*, 'Gender differences and factors related to the disposition toward cohabitation', *Family Therapy*, Vol. 21, 1994, pp. 171-84.

30   Sarantakos, 'Trial cohabitation on trial', 1994.

31   McAllister, F., *Marital Breakdown and the Health of the Nation*, London: One Plus One, 1995, p. 6.

32   Lillard, L.A. and Waite, L.J., 'Til death do us part: marital disruption and mortality', *American Journal of Sociology*, Vol. 100, 1995, p. 1131.

33   McAllister, *Marital Breakdown and the Health of the Nation* 1995.

34   Svedin, C.G. and Wadsby, M., 'The presence of psychiatric consultations in relation to divorce', *Acta Psychiatrica Scandinavica*, Vol. 5, 1998, pp. 414-22.

35   McAllister, *Marital Breakdown and the Health of the Nation*, 1995.

36   Larsen, D.B., Swyers, J.P. and Larson, S.S., *The Costly Consequences of Divorce: Assessing the Clinical, Economic and Public Health Impact of Marital Disruption in the United States*, Rockvill MD: National Centre for Healthcare Research, 46, 1995; and Lee, S.H. *et al.*, *Health Differentials Among Working Age Australians*, Canberra: Australian Institute of Health, 1987. National Health Strategy, *Enough to Make You Sick: How Income and Environment Effect Health*, Australian Institute of Health, 1992.

37   Lillard and Waite, 'Til death do us part: marital disruption and mortality', 1995.

38   Booth, A. and Johnson, D., 'Pre-marital cohabitation and marital success', *Journal of Family Issues*, Vol. 9, 1988, pp. 255-72.

39   Goldman, N., 'Marriage selection and mortality patterns: inferences and fallacies', *Demography*, Vol. 30, No. 2, 1993, pp. 189-208.

40   *To Have and To Hold: A Report of the Inquiry into Aspects of Family Services*, House of Representatives Standing Committee on Legal and Constitutional Affairs, Canberra, June 1998.

41   Lillard, L.A. and Panis, C.W.A., 'Marital status and mortality: the role of health', *Demography*, Vol. 33, No. 3, August 1996, pp. 313-27.

42   Lillard and Waite, 'Til death do us part: marital disruption and mortality', 1995.

43   Umberson, D., 'Family status and health behaviours: social control as a dimension of social integration', *Journal of Health and Social Behaviour*, Vol. 28, 1987, pp. 306-19.

44   Sclone, B.S. and Weinick, R.M., 'Health related behaviours and the benefits of marriage for elderly persons', *Gerontologist*, Vol. 38, No. 5, 1998, pp. 618-27.

45   Umberson, 'Family status and health behaviours: social control as a dimension of social integration', 1987.

46   Evidence from General Household Survey quoted by McAllister (McAllister, *Marital Breakdown and the Health of the Nation*, 1995) is that nearly one in seven or 14 per cent of divorced/

separated men drink dangerous levels of alcohol, or over 50
units a week, compared to four per cent of married men.

47   Sarantakos, *Living Together in Australia*, 1984 p. 138.

48   Horwitz, A.V. and White, H.R., 'The relationship of cohabitation
      and mental health: a study of a young adult cohort', *Journal of
      Marriage and the Family*, Vol. 60, 1998, pp. 505-14.

49   Horwitz and White, 'The relationship of cohabitation and
      mental health: a study of a young adult cohort', p. 512.

50   Mastekaasa, A., 'Marital status, distress and well-being: an
      international comparison', *Journal of Comparative Family
      Studies*, Vol. 25, No. 2, 1994, p. 183.

51   Kurdek, L. A., The relations between reported well-being and
      divorce history, availability of a proximate adult, and gender',
      Journal of Marriage and the Family, Vol. 53, February 1991, pp.
      71-78.

52   Robins, L. and Reiger, D., *Psychiatric Disorders in America*,
      New York: Free Press, 1990; and see Horwitz and White, 'The
      relationship of cohabitation and mental health: a
      study of a young adult cohort', 1995.

53   In Wisconsin, Ladbrook, D., 'Sex differentials in premature
      death among profesionals', *Journal of the Australian Population
      Association*, Vol. 7, 1990, pp. 1-28; 89-115.

54   The Advisory Board on Family Law, *Second Annual Report*,
      Lord Chancellor's Office, 1998/99, p. 14.

55   Kiernan, K. and Mueller, G., *The Divorced and Who Divorces?*,
      CASEpaper CASE/7, 1998, Centre for Analysis of Social
      Exclusion, May 1998.

56   Waite, L.J., 'Does marriage matter?', *Demography*, Vol. 32, No.
      4, November 1995, pp. 483-507; and Daniel, K., 'The marriage
      premium', in Tommasi, M. and Ierulli, K. (eds.), *The New
      Economics of Human Behaviour*, Cambridge UK: Cambridge
      University Press, 1996.

57   Korenman, S.D. and Neumark, D., *Does Marriage Really Make
      Men More Productive?*, Finance and Economics Discussion
      Series, No. 29, Washington DC: Division of Research and
      Statistics, Federal Reserve Board, May 1988.

58   Sarantakos, *Living Together in Australia*, 1984.

59   Wellings, K., Field, J., Johnson, A., Wadsworth, J., *Sexual
      Behaviour in Britain: The National Survey of Sexual Attitudes
      and Lifestyles*, London: Penguin Books, 1994, p. 116.

60   Steinhaiser, J., 'No marriage, no apologies', *New York Times*, 6
      July 1995.

61 Wellings, *et al.*, *Sexual Behaviour in Britain,* 1994, p. 116.

62 Wellings, *et al.*, *Sexual Behaviour in Britain,* 1994; and *Living in Britain: Results for the 1995 General Household Survey*, Office for National Statistics, London: HMSO, 1997.

63 Sarantakos, *Living Together in Australia,* 1984, p. 128.

64 Rindfuss, R.R. and Vandenheuvel, A., 'Cohabitation: a precursor to marriage or an alternative to being single?', *Population and Development Review*, Vol. 40, 1990, pp. 703-26.

65 Smart, C. and Stevens, P., *Cohabitation Breakdown*, London: Family Policy Studies Centre, 2000, pp. 23, 33.

Chapter 5: The Outcomes For Children

1 Schuman, J., 'Childhood, infant and perinatal mortality, 1996: social and biological factors in deaths of children aged under 3', *Population Trends*, Vol. 92, Summer 1998.

2 Daly, M. and Wilson, M., *The Truth About Cinderella: A Darwinian View of Parental Love*, London: Weidenfeld and Nicholson, 1998. In US data, children under two have a hundred times greater risk of being killed by step-parents than by genetic parents; in Canadian data the risk is 70 fold. The increased risk cannot be attributed to reporting or detection bias, maternal youth, family size, poverty, or other social factors that have been associated with child abuse. See also, Malkin, C.M. and Lamb, M.E., 'Child maltreatment: a test of sociobiological theory', *Journal of Comparative Family Studies*, Vol. 25, 1994, pp. 121-30. Out of 52,000 child abuse cases 72 per cent involved children in a household without one or both biological parents, even though such households comprise roughly a third of all households with children. Smith, C. and Thornberry, T.P., 'The relationship between childhood maltreatment and adolescent involvement in delinquency', *Criminology*, Vol. 33, 1995, pp. 451-79. Only 3.2 per cent of children raised with both biological parents had a history of maltreatment, compared with 18.6 per cent in other family situations.

3 Honess, T.M. *et al.*, 'Conflict between parents and adolescents: variation by family constitution', *British Journal of Developmental Psychology*, Vol. 15, 1997, pp. 367-85.

4 Whelan, R., *Broken Homes and Battered Children: A Study of the Relationship Between Child Abuse and Family Type,* Oxford: Family Education Trust, 1993.

5 Evans, A., *We Don't Choose to be Homeless*, London: CHAR (now National Homeless Alliance), 1996; Smith, J., Gilford, S. and O'Sullivan, A., *The Family Backgrounds of Homeless Young People*, London: Family Policy Studies Centre, 1998; also see

Jones, G., *Leaving Home*, Open University Press, 1995; and Strathdee, R., *No Way Back*, London: Centrepoint, 1992.

6   McLanahan, S.S. and Sandefur, G., *Growing Up With a Single Parent*, Cambridge, Mass: Harvard University Press, 1994.

7   Sarantakos, S., 'Children in three contexts: family, education and social development', *Children Australia*, Vol. 21, No. 3, 1996.

8   Sarantakos, 'Children in three contexts: family, education and social development', 1996, p. 29.

9   Sarantakos, S., 'Cohabitation, marriage and delinquency: the significance of family environment', *Australian and New Zealand Journal of Criminology*, Vol. 30, No. 2,1997, pp. 187-99.

10   Sarantakos, S., 'The virtues of liberation: a sequel to Kevin Andrews', *Threshold*, Vol. 5, 1996, pp. 9-11.

11   Meltzer, H. *et al.*, *Mental Health of Children and Adolescents in Great Britain*, Office for National Statistics, London: The Stationery Office, 2000. The results match those from the western Australian Survey of 14,100 children. Zubrick, S.R. *et al.*, *Western Australian Child Health Survey: Education, Health and Competence*, Perth, Western Australia: Australian Bureau of Statistics and the TVW Institute for Child Health Research, 1995.

12   US Bureau of the Census, *Marriage, Divorce and Remarriage in the 1990s*, Current Population Reports Series P-22, No. 180, Washington DC: US Government Printing Office, 1992; and see Zill, N. and Rogers, C.C., 'Recent trends in the well-being of children in the United States and their implications for public policy', in Cherlin, A. (ed.), *The Changing American Family and Public Policy*, Washington DC: Urban Institute Press.

13   Sarantakos, 'The virtues of liberation: A sequel to Kevin Andrews',1996.

Chapter 6: No Trial Run For Commitment

1   Willis, R.J. and Michael, R.T., 'Innovation in family formation: Evidence on cohabitation in the United States', in Ermisch, J. and Ogawa, N. (eds.), *The Family, the Market, and the State in Ageing Societies*, Oxford: Clarendon Press, 1994, p. 10.

2   Waite, L.J., 'Does marriage matter?', *Demography*, Vol. 32, No. 4, November 1995, pp. 483-507.

3   McClean, M. and Eekelaar, J., *The Parental Obligation*, Oxford: Hart Publishing, 1997, p. 8.

4   *To Have and To Hold:, A Report of the Inquiry into Aspects of Family Services*, House of Representatives Standing Committee on Legal and Constitutional Affairs, Canberra, June 1998, p. 31.

5   Becker, G.S., *A Treatise on the Family*, Cambridge, Mass: Harvard University Press, 1991.

6   Eurostat, *Women and Men in the European Union: A Statistical Portrait*, Luxembourg: Office for Official Publications of the European Communities, 1995; also see Kiernan, K., *European Perspectives on Non-marital Childbearing*, Department of Social Policy and Centre for Analysis of Social Exclusion, London School of Economics, paper prepared for Conference on Non-marital Childbearing, Madison, Wisconsin, 29-30 April 1999.

7   Pickford, R., *Fathers, Marriage, and the Law*, London: Family Policy Studies Centre, 1999.

8   McRae, S., *Cohabiting Mothers: Changing Marriage and Motherhood?*, London: Policy Studies Institute, 1993, p. 8.

9   Johnson, M.P. in Jones, W.H. and Perlam, D. (eds.), *Advances in Personal Relationships: A Research Manual*, London: Jessica Kinsley, 1991.

10   Mansfield, P., 'Commitment: Who Cares?', Opening Remarks, Proceedings of the One Plus One Marriage and Partnership Research Conference, 25 October 1999, p. 5.

11   Kurdek, L.A., 'Relationship outcomes and their predictors: longitudinal evidence from heterosexual married, gay cohabiting, and lesbian cohabiting couples', *Journal of Marriage and the Family*, Vol. 60, August 1998, pp. 553-68.

12   Adams, J.M. and Jones, W.H., 'The conceptualisation of marital commitment: An integrative analysis.' *Journal of Personality and Social Psychology*, Vol. 72, 1997, pp. 1177-96.

13   Pickford, *Fathers, Marriage, and the Law*, 1999, p. 39.

14   Mansfield, 'Commitment: Who Cares?', 1999, p. 8.

15   Mansfield, 'Commitment: Who Cares?', 1999, p. 9.

16   Mansfield, 'Commitment: Who Cares?', 1999, pp.7-8.

17   Nock, S.L., 'A comparison of marriages and cohabiting relationships', *Journal of Family Issues*, Vol. 16, 1995, pp. 53-76.

18   Axinn, W.G. and Thornton, A., 'Pre-marital cohabitation and divorce: selectivity or causal influence?', *Demography*, Vol. 29, 1992, pp. 357-74.

19   Clarkberg, M., Stolzenberg, R.M. and Waite, L.J., 'Attitudes, values, and entrance into cohabitational versus marital unions', *Social Forces*, Vol. 74, No. 2, 1995, p. 610.

20   Sarantakos, S., Living Together in Australia, Melbourne: Longman Cheshire, 1984.

21   Dench, G., *The Place of Men in Changing Family Cultures*,
      London: Institute of Community Studies, 1996, p. 59.

22   Sarantakos, *Living Together in Australia*, 1984, p. 95.

23   Gallagher, M., *The Abolition of Marriage,* Washington DC:
      Regnery, 1996, p. 168.

24   Waite, L.J., 'Cohabitation: a communitarian perspective', paper
      presented to the Communitarian Task Force, Washington, DC,
      January 1999.

25   Sarantakos, S., 'Trial cohabitation on trial', *Australian Social
      Work*, Vol. 47, No.3, 1994, p. 24.

26   Carlson, A., 'Liberty, Order and the Family', in Davies, J. (ed.),
      The Family: Is It Just Another Lifestyle Choice?, London: IEA
      Health and Welfare Unit, p. 53.

27   Nock, 'A comparison of marriages and cohabiting relationships',
      1995.

28   Nock, 'A comparison of marriages and cohabiting relationships',
      1995, p. 143.

29   Daly, M. and Wilson, M., *Homicide,* New York: Aldine de
      Gruyter, 1988, p. 187.

30   Brown, S.L. and Booth, A., 'Cohabitation versus marriage: a
      comparison of relationship quality', *Journal of Marriage and the
      Family*, Vol. 58, No. 3, 1996, pp. 668-78.

31   Adams, J.M. and Jones, W.H., 'The conceptualisation of marital
      commitment: An integrative analysis', *Journal of Personality
      and Social Psychology*, Vol. 72, 1997, pp. 1177-96.

32   Adams and Jones, 'The conceptualisation of marital
      commitment: An integrative analysis', 1997, p. 1187.

33   Nock, 'A comparison of marriages and cohabiting relationships',
      1995.

34   Berger, P.L. and Berger, B., *The War Over the Family*, London:
      Hutchinson, 1983.

Chapter 7: In Search Of What?

1   Pickford, R., *Fathers, Marriage, and the Law*, London: Family
      Policy Studies Centre, 1999.

2   Sarantakos, S., *Living Together in Australia*, Melbourne:
      Longman Cheshire, 1984, p. 185.

3   Wilson, J.Q., in Whelan, R. (ed.), *Just a Piece of Paper? Divorce
      Reform and the Undermining of Marriage*, London: IEA Health
      and Welfare Unit, 1995, p. 87.

4   Smart, C. and Stevens, P., *Cohabitation Breakdown*, London: Family Policy Studies Centre, 2000, p. 33.

5   Sarantakos, S., 'Trial cohabitation on trial', *Australian Social Work*, September 1994, Vol. 47, No. 3 p. 13.

6   Sarantakos, 'Trial cohabitation on trial', 1994, p. 64.

7   Bumpass, L.L., Sweet, J.A. and Cherlin, A., 'The role of cohabitation in declining rates of marriage', *Journal of Marriage and the Family*, Vol. 53, 1991, pp. 913-27.

8   Bumpass, Sweet and Cherlin, 'The role of cohabitation in declining rates of marriage', 1991, p. 923.

9   Bumpass, Sweet and Cherlin, 'The role of cohabitation in declining rates of marriage', 1991.

10   Smart and Stevens, *Cohabitation Breakdown*, 2000.

11   Sarantakos, S., *Living Together in Australia*, Melbourne: Longman Cheshire, 1984, p. 105.

12   Sarantakos, *Living Together in Australia*, 1984, p. 144.

13   Whitehead, B.D. and Popenoe, D., 'Sex without strings, relationships without rings', *The State of Our Unions, The Social Health of Marriage in America*, The National Marriage Project, Rutgers, The State University of New Jersey, 2000, p. 13. [http://marriage.rutgers.edu]

14   Stets, J.E. and Straus, M.A., 'The marriage license as a hitting license: a comparison of assaults in dating, cohabiting, and married couples', in Straus, M.A. and Gelles, R.J., *Physical Violence in American Families*, New Jersey: Transaction, 1995, p. 242.

15   Blankenhorn, D., *Fatherless America*, New York: Basic Books, 1995, p. 36.

Chapter 8: Living Down To Expectations

1   Booth, A. and Johnson, D. 'Pre-marital cohabitation and marital success', *Journal of Family Issues*, Vol. 9, 1988, pp. 255-72.

2   Pickford, R., *Fathers, Marriage, and the Law*, London: Family Policy Studies Centre, 1999, p. 42.

3   Clarkberg, M., Stolzenberg, R.M. and Waite, L.J., 'Attitudes, values, and entrance into cohabitational versus marital unions', *Social Forces*, Vol. 74, No. 2, 1995, pp. 609-32.

4   Clarkberg, Stolzenberg and Waite, 'Attitudes, values, and entrance into cohabitational versus marital unions', 1995, p. 623.

5   Axinn, W.G. and Thornton, A., 'Pre-marital cohabitation and
         divorce: selectivity or causal influence?', *Demography*, Vol. 29,
         1992, pp. 357-74.

6   Clarkberg, Stolzenberg and Waite, 'Attitudes, values, and
         entrance into cohabitational versus marital unions', 1995.

7   Axinn and Thornton, 'Pre-marital cohabitation and divorce:
         selectivity or causal influence?', 1992.

8   Axinn and Thornton, 'Pre-marital cohabitation and divorce:
         selectivity or causal influence?', 1992.

9   Amato, P.R. and Booth, A., *A Generation at Risk*, Cambridge,
         Mass: Harvard University Press, 1997.

10   Kiernan, K., 'Cohabitation in Western Europe', *Population
         Trends*, Vol. 96, Office for National Statistics, 1999.

11   Kiernan, 'Cohabitation in Western Europe', 1999, p. 40.

12   Kiernan, K., *European Perspectives on Non-marital
         Childbearing*, Department of Social Policy and Centre for
         Analysis of Social Exclusion, London School of Economics, paper
         prepared for Conference on Non-marital Childbearing, Madison,
         Wisconsin, 29-30 April 1999.

13   Amato and Booth, *A Generation at Risk*, 1997, p. 113.

14   Glezer, H., 'To tie or not tie the knot: pathways to family
         formation', Paper presented to the Fourth Australian Family
         Research Conference, Sydney, 1993.

15   Blom, S., 'Marriage and cohabitation in a changing society:
         experience of Norwegian men and women born in 1945 and
         1960', *European Journal of Population*, Vol. 9, 1994, pp. 143-73;
         and Khoo, S-E., *Living Together: Young Couples in De Facto
         Relationships*, Melbourne: Collins Dove for the Australian
         Institute of Family Studies, 1986.

16   Amato and Booth, *A Generation at Risk*, 1997, p. 113.

17   Sarantakos, S., *Living Together in Australia*, Melbourne:
         Longman Cheshire, 1984.

18   Booth and Johnson, 'Pre-marital cohabitation and marital
         success', 1988.

19   Carmichael, G.A., 'Consensual partnering in the more developed
         countries', *Journal of the Australian Population Association* Vol.
         12, No. 1, 1995, p. 67.

20   Leridon, H., 'Extra-marital cohabitation and fertility',
         Population Studies, Vol. 44, 1990, pp. 469-87.

21   *Australian Family Formation Study*, Melbourne: Australian
         Institute of Family Studies, 1991.

22   Hoem, B., 'Early phases of family formation in contemporary
        Sweden', CDE Working Paper 88-44, Centre for Demography
        and Ecology, University of Wisconsin, Madison, p. 11.

23   Glezer, 'To tie or not tie the knot: pathways to family formation',
        1993.

24   Sarantakos, *Living Together in Australia*, 1984.

25   See Carmichael, 'Consensual partnering in the more developed
        countries', 1995.

26   Schoen, R. and Weinick, R.M., 'Partner choice in marriage and
        cohabitation', *Journal of Marriage and the Family*, Vol. 55,
        1993, pp. 408-14.

27   Rindfuss, R.R. and VandenHeuvel. A., 'Cohabitation: a
        precursor to marriage, or an alternative to being single?',
        Population and Development Review, Vol. 14, No. 4, 1990, p.
        723.

28   Thomson, E. and Colella, U., 'Cohabitation and marital
        stability: quality or commitment?', *Journal of Marriage and the
        Family*, Vol. 54, 1992, pp. 259-67.

29   Kurdek, L. A., 'Predicting marital dissolution: a 5-year
        prospective longitudinal study of newlywed couples', *Journal of
        Personality and Social Psychology*, Vol. 64, No. 2, 1993, p. 240.

30   Clarke, L. and Berrington, A., 'Socio-demographic predictors of
        divorce', in Simons, J. (ed.), *High Divorce Rates: The State of the
        Evidence on Reasons and Remedies*, Research series No. 2/99,
        Vol. 1, 1999, Lord Chancellor's Department, p. 17.

31   Cunningham, J.D. and Antill, J.K., 'Cohabitation and marriage:
        retrospective and predictive comparisons', *Journal of Social and
        Personal Relationships*, Vol. 11, 1994, pp. 77-93.

32   Axinn, W.G. and Barber, J.S., 'Living arrangements and family
        formation attitudes in early adulthood', *Journal of Marriage
        and the Family*, Vol. 59, 1997, pp. 595-611.

33   Hall, D.R., 'Marriage as a pure relationship: exploring the link
        between pre-marital cohabitation and divorce in Canada',
        Journal of Comparative Family Studies, Vol. XXVII, No. 1,
        Spring 1996.

34   Sarantakos, S., 'Trial cohabitation on trial', *Australian Social
        Work*, Vol. 47, No. 3, 1994.

35   Popenoe, D. and Whitehead, B.D., *Should We Live Together?
        What Young Adults Need To Know about Cohabitation before
        Marriage*, The National Marriage Project, Rutgers, The State
        University of New Jersey, Brunswick, New Jersey, 1999, p. 5.

36   Clarke and Berrington, 'Socio-demographic predictors of
        divorce', 1999.

37   Axinn and Barber, 'Living arrangements and family formation
        attitudes in early adulthood', 1997.

Chapter 9: Afraid To Love Without A Net

1   Sarantakos, S., 'Trial cohabitation on trial', *Australian Social
        Work*, Vol. 47, No. 3, 1994, pp. 13-25.

2   Popenoe, D. and Whitehead, B.D., *Should We Live Together?
        What Young Adults Need To Know about Cohabitation before
        Marriage*, The National Marriage Project, Rutgers, The State
        University of New Jersey, Brunswick, New Jersey, 1999, p. 5.

3   Sarantakos, 'Trial cohabitation on trial', 1994.

4   Popenoe and Whitehead, *Should We Live Together?*, 1999.

5   Clarke, L. and Berrington, A., 'Socio-demographic predictors of
        divorce', in Simons, J. (ed.), *High Divorce Rates: The State of the
        Evidence on Reasons and Remedies*, Research series No.2/99,
        Vol. 1, Lord Chancellor's Department, 1999, p. 17.

6   'Children's needs, coping strategies and understanding of
        woman abuse', *Children 5-16: Research Briefing No. 12*,
        Economic and Social Research Council, Department of Applied
        Social Sciences, University of Stirling, Stirling, April 2000.

7   Ringen, S., *The Family In Question*, London: Demos pp. 46-47.

8   Gallagher, M., *The Abolition of Marriage,* Washington DC:
        Regnery, 1996, p. 168.

9   See Whitehead, B.D. and Popenoe, D., 'Sex without strings,
        relationships without rings', *The State of Our Unions, The
        Social Health of Marriage in America*, The National Marriage
        Project, Rutgers, The State University of New Jersey, 2000.
        [http://marriage.rutgers.edu]

10   Gallagher, *The Abolition of Marriage*, 1996, p. 168.

11   Carmichael, G.A., 'Consensual partnering in the more developed
        countries', *Journal of the Australian Population Association*,
        Vol. 12, No. 1, 1995, p. 69.

12   Carmichael, 'Consensual partnering in the more developed
        countries', 1995, p. 79.

13   Kramer, P.D., *Should You Leave?*, London:Victor Gollancz, the
        Cassell Group, 1998, p. 77.

14   Kramer, *Should You Leave?*, 1998.

15   Sarantakos, S., *Living Together in Australia*, Melbourne:
        Longman Cheshire, 1984, p. 107.

16   Giddens, A., *The Transformation of Intimacy*, Stanford: Stanford
        University Press, 1992, p. 136.

17   Parker, S., *Informal Marriage, Cohabitation and the Law, 1750-1989*, London: Macmillan, 1990, p. 16.

18   Axinn, W.G. and Thornton, A., 'Pre-marital cohabitation and divorce: selectivity or causal influence?', *Demography*, Vol. 29, 1992, pp. 357-74.

19   Axinn, W.G. and Barber, J.S., 'Living arrangements and family formation attitudes in early adulthood', *Journal of Marriage and the Family*, Vol. 59, 1997, pp. 595-611.

20   Amato, P.R. and Booth, A., *A Generation at Risk*, Cambridge, Mass: Harvard University Press, 1997, pp. 118-19.

21   Dench, G., *The Place of Men in Changing Family Cultures*, London: Institute of Community Studies, 1996, p. 60.

22   Blankenhorn, D., *Fatherless America,* New York: Basic Books, 1995, p. 36.

23   Goldscheider, F.K. and Kaufman, G., 'Fertility and commitment: bringing men back in', presented at the Workshop on Expanding Frameworks for Fertility Research in Industrialised Countries, National Research Council, Woods Hole, MA, 1994, p. 3. See also Jones, G.W., 'Review of William J. Goode, *World Changes in Divorce Patterns*', *Population and Development Review*, 20, 1994, pp. 899-901.

24   Ermisch, J., *Personal communication,* December 1999.

Chapter 10: Why Discriminate Against Cohabitation?

1   *1. Court Procedures for the Determination of Paternity 2. The Law on Parental responsibility for Unmarried Fathers*, Lord Chancellor's Department, March 1988, p. 3.

2   The Advisory Board on Family Law, *Second Annual Report*, Lord Chancellor's Office, 1998/99, p. 22. However, the weight attached to this 'commitment' can be gauged by the fact that the Board considered that parental responsibility acquired through joint birth registration should be only provisional or still revocable by the court, not least since 'an unmarried mother might be more reluctant to encourage her partner to register the birth jointly if she knew that he would thereby acquire parental responsibility irrevocably' (p. 23). Ominously, this led to the 'question whether the courts should be given new powers to revoke parental responsibility even when it had been acquired automatically by married parents or an unmarried mother', in that there would remain a distinction between married fathers and unmarried mothers on the one hand and unmarried fathers on the other, which would leave the UK vulnerable to allegations of discrimination under the UN Convention on Human Rights. The Board did not think it desirable that the responsibility of married parents should be revocable by the court.

3   Pickford, R., *Fathers, Marriage, and the Law*, London: Family Policy Studies Centre, 1999, p. 45.

4   Pickford, *Fathers, Marriage, and the Law*, 1999.

5   McRae, S., *Cohabiting Mothers: Changing Marriage and Motherhood?*, London: Policy Studies Institute, 1993 p. 9.

6   Pickford, *Fathers, Marriage, and the Law*, 1999, p. 45.

7   Gallagher, M., *The Abolition of Marriage,* Washington DC: Regnery, 1996, p. 7.

8   Letter from David Lloyd, Head of News, Current Affairs and Business, Channel Four Television, to Robert Whiston, 11 December 1998.

9   McClean, M. and Eekelaar, J., *The Parental Obligation*, Oxford: Hart Publishing, 1997, p. 147.

10   Parker, S., *Informal Marriage, Cohabitation and the Law, 1750-1989*, London: Macmillan, 1990.

11   Parker, *Informal Marriage*, 1990, p. 97.

12   Davis, E. and Phillips, M., *A Fruitless Marriage? Same-sex Couples and Partnership Rights*, London: Social Market Foundation, 1999.

13   McLanahan, S.S. and Sandefur, G., *Growing Up With a Single Parent*, Cambridge, Mass: Harvard University Press, 1994, p. 3.

14   Gallagher, *The Abolition of Marriage*, 1996, p. 243.

15   Mansfield, P., 'Commitment: Who Cares?', Discussion, Proceedings of the One Plus One Marriage and Partnership Research Conference, 25 October 1999, p. 19. See also Parish, T.S. and Necessary, J.R., 'Parents' actions: are they related to children's self-concepts, evaluations of parents and to each other?', *Adolescence*, Vol. 29, No. 116, Winter 1994, pp. 943-47.

16   Smart, C. and Stevens, P., *Cohabitation Breakdown*, London: Family Policy Studies Centre, 2000, p. 37.

17   Rodgers, B. and Pryor, J., *Divorce and Separation: The Outcomes for Children,* York: Joseph Rowntree Foundation, 1998.

18   Benefits may depend on whether parents get along, otherwise positive and negative effects cancel each other out. Rodgers and Pryor, *Divorce and Separation*, 1998.

19   Amato, P.R. and Booth, A., *A Generation at Risk*, Cambridge, Mass: Harvard University Press, 1997, p. 119.

20   *The Merits of Marriage*, London: CARE (Christian Action for Research and Education), Public Policy Department, 1998.

21 Sarantakos, S., *Living Together in Australia*, Melbourne: Longman Cheshire, 1984, p. 187.

22 Pickford, *Fathers, Marriage, and the Law*, 1999, p. 25.

23 Pickford, *Fathers, Marriage, and the Law*, 1999, p. 33.

24 Pickford, *Fathers, Marriage, and the Law*, 1999, p. 35.

25 Pickford, *Fathers, Marriage, and the Law*, 1999, pp. 25, 40.

26 Smart, and Stevens, *Cohabitation Breakdown*, 2000, p. 47.

27 Sarantakos, *Living Together in Australia*, 1984, p. 193.

28 Gallagher, *The Abolition of Marriage*, 1996, p. 141.

29 Fineman, M.A., *The Neutered Mother and the Sexual Family*, New York: Routledge, 1995, p. 229.

30 'Cohabitation Proposals for Reform of the Law', Family Law Committee of the Law Society, 1999.

31 See Phillips M., in Davis, E. and Phillips, M., *A Fruitless Marriage?*, London: Social Market Foundation 1999.

32 Maley, B., *Marriage, Divorce and Family Justice*, St Leonards Australia: The Centre of Independent Studies, Policy Monograph 25, 1992.

33 Maley, *Marriage, Divorce and Family Justice*, 1992, p. 19.

34 Gallagher, *The Abolition of Marriage*, 1996, p. 171.

35 McRae, *Cohabiting Mothers: Changing Marriage and Motherhood?*, 1993, p. 102.

36 Gallagher, *The Abolition of Marriage*, 1996, p. 171.

37 Smart and Stevens, *Cohabitation Breakdown*, 2000, p. 44.

38 Bloom, A., *The Closing of the American Mind*, Simon and Schuster, 1987, p. 175.

Chapter 11: Back To The Future ... Not

1 McRae, S., *Cohabiting Mothers: Changing Marriage and Motherhood?*, London: Policy Studies Institute, 1993, p. 150.

2 McRae, *Cohabiting Mothers*, 1993, p. 6.

3 Sarantakos, S., *Living Together in Australia*, Melbourne: Longman Cheshire, 1984, p. 153.

4 Parker, S., *Informal Marriage, Cohabitation and the Law, 1750-1989*, London: Macmillan, 1990, p. 19.

5 Parker, *Informal Marriage,* 1990, p. 19.

6 Parker, *Informal Marriage,* 1990, p. 20.

7 Parker, *Informal Marriage,* 1990, p. 26.

8   Davis, K., 'The meaning and significance of marriage in
         contemporary society', in Davis, K. (ed.), *Contemporary
         Marriage: Comparative Perspectives on a Changing Institution*,
         New York: Russell Sage Foundation, c.1985, pp. 7-8.

9   Davis, 'The meaning and significance of marriage in
         contemporary society', p. 35.

10   Davis, 'The meaning and significance of marriage in
         contemporary society', p. 46, quoting from William Cobbett,
         Parliamentary History.

11   Davis, 'The meaning and significance of marriage in
         contemporary society', p. 78.

12   Whitehead, B.D. and Popenoe, D., 'Sex without strings,
         relationships without rings', *The State of Our Unions*, *The
         Social Health of Marriage in America*, The National Marriage
         Project, Rutgers, The State University of New Jersey, 2000, p.
         15. [http://marriage.rutgers.edu]

13   Grove, V., 'Marriage, who needs it?', Interview with Ed Straw,
         Chairman of Relate, *The Times*, 5 February 2000.

14   Wetzstein, C., 'Experts concerned about social costs of family
         collapse', *The Washington Times*, 9 December 1998; and see
         Glenn, N., *Closed Hearts, Closed Minds: the Textbook Story of
         Marriage*, New York: Institute for American Values, 1997.

Chapter 12: The Meaning Of Marriage

1   Sarantakos, S., 'Trial cohabitation on trial', *Australian Social
         Work*, Vol. 47, No. 3, 1994, pp. 13-25.

2   *The State of Our Unions*, *The Social Health of Marriage in
         America*, The National Marriage Project, Rutgers, The State
         University of New Jersey, 1999, p. 13.

3   *1. Court Procedures for the Determination of Paternity 2. The
         Law on Parental Responsibility for Unmarried Fathers,* Lord
         Chancellor's Department, March 1988, p. 16.

4   Rawls. J., *A Theory of Justice*, Cambridge, Mass: Harvard
         University Press, 1971, pp. 55-56.

5   Maley, B., *Marriage, Divorce and Family Justice*, St Leonards,
         Australia: The Centre of Independent Studies, Policy
         Monograph 25, 1992, pp. 18-19.

6   Logan, B., *Marriage: Do We Need It?*, Christchurch, NZ: New
         Zealand Education Foundation, p. 32.

7   See Gallagher, M., *The Abolition of Marriage,* Washington DC:
         Regnery, 1996.

8   A Gallop poll asked a cross-section of 660 people, 'Should
        children be taught that marriage is a good thing?, 75 per cent
        said yes and 19 per cent said no. *Corporal Punishment Poll*, 12
        November 1996, Gallup.

9   The Review of the national curriculum in England: The
        Secretary of State's Proposals, May-July 1999, Department of
        Education.

10   *The State of Our Unions, The Social Health of Marriage in
        America*, The National Marriage Project, Rutgers, The State
        University of New Jersey, 1999.

11   Present understanding of commitment may be so crass that, in
        one study, a man defined this as 'basically me being able to do
        what I want and get away with it'. Smart, C. and Stevens, P.,
        Cohabitation Breakdown, London: Family Policy Studies
        Centre, 2000, p. 33.

12   Popenoe, D and Whitehead, B.D. *Should We Live Together?
        What young adults need to know about cohabitation before
        marriage.* The National Marriage Project. Rutgers, The State
        University of New Jersey. Brunswick: New Jersey, 1999.

13   Whitehead, B.D. and Popenoe, D., 'Sex without strings,
        relationships without rings', *The State of Our Unions, The
        Social Health of Marriage in America*, The National Marriage
        Project, Rutgers, The State University of New Jersey, 2000.
        [http://marriage.rutgers.edu]

14   Sarantakos, 'Trial cohabitation on trial', 1994.

118

Index